Christmas Scrapcrafts

Christmas Scrapcrafts

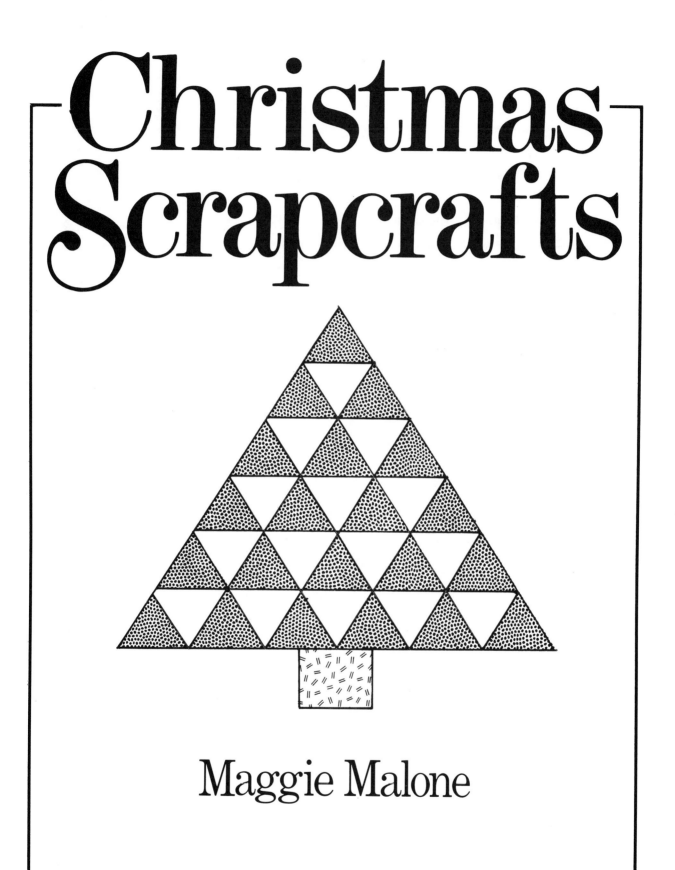

Maggie Malone

Sterling Publishing Co., Inc.   New York

Library of Congress Cataloging-in-Publication Data
Malone, Maggie
    Christmas scrapcrafts / Maggie Malone.
        p.   cm.
    Includes index.
    ISBN 0-8069-6804-4
    1. Patchwork.   2. Christmas decorations.   I. Title.
TT835.M272   1991
746.46—dc20   91–23273
                                                    CIP

10   9   8   7   6   5   4   3   2   1

Published by Sterling Publishing Company, Inc.
387 Park Avenue South, New York, N.Y. 10016
Distributed in Canada by Sterling Publishing
℅ Canadian Manda Group, P.O. Box 920, Station U
Toronto, Ontario, Canada M8Z 5P9
Distributed in Great Britain and Europe by Cassell PLC
Villiers House, 41/47 Strand, London WC2N 5JE, England
Distributed in Australia by Capricorn Ltd.
P.O. Box 665, Lane Cove, NSW 2066
Manufactured in the United States of America

Sterling ISBN 0-8069-6804-4

Contents

GIFTS

INDEX   126

Foreword

If you've been sewing for any length of time, you probably have the same problem I have: a mountain of scraps. You know, those pieces that were just too big to throw away, that you'll use "someday."

My someday came the day my children ransacked my sewing room, scattering bits and pieces of fabric everywhere. To give you some idea of the mess: I've been sewing for close to thirty years, and I think the only fabric I didn't save was from my very first project.

In addition to the sewing scraps I also had a stack of fabric lengths I had picked up over the years and once home, never found a use for. I would look at some of them and wonder whatever possessed me to buy them in the first place. Oh yes, and let's not forget the baskets of outgrown or out-of-date clothing. (I'm a pack rat at heart; just can't seem to throw anything away.)

Being a quilter, my first thought was to use all the cotton scraps for quilts. I cut out fourteen scrap patterns and still hadn't made a dent in the pile. Something more drastic was required.

So I began experimenting, with place mats, tablecloths, pillows, curtains, boxes, baskets and bags of all sorts, covers for just about everything in my house, folding screens, fireplace screens, and on and on.

In the following pages you will find instructions for many of these projects done in a wide variety of techniques. The instructions given will duplicate the project shown. However, I found that as I would work with a particular technique I thought of another way it could be used, and in those instances I've included hints and suggestions for you to change or adapt the technique to satisfy your own creative urges.

Now, on to the projects. I hope you have as much fun making them as I did.

—Maggie Malone

SCRAP QUILTS

Scrap quilts are an excellent way to satisfy the thrifty side in all of us. By investing just a "little" time we get something beautiful for almost nothing.

Fabrics

Cotton is the preferred fabric for quilt-making because it is easy to sew and quilt, but with a little knowledge of techniques you can use just about any kind of fabric you have, from denim to corduroy, to silks and satins to polyester knits.

Denim, corduroy and sport-weight cottons can be quickly sewn on the machine. Choose large, simple designs with a minimum of seams for these heavyweights. A pattern like *Autumn Tints* would be a good choice. Finish off by tying the three layers together for a quick-to-make, heavy-duty comforter that will stand up to the wear and tear of kids.

Silks and satins can be used for quilts that will not be subjected to a lot of hard wear, although their durability can be increased by using an iron-on interfacing on the back of each piece. This will prevent ravelling and add stability to the pieces. Such quilts can be tied or quilted as desired.

Templates

To make templates, first trace the pattern pieces in the book onto another sheet of paper. This is then transferred to cardboard, using carbon paper. Make several patterns because there is wear as you trace around them, and this could result in inaccuracies in your fabric pieces. File folders are excellent for durable patterns. Soapboxes made from heavy cardboard are also good for making patterns. Another choice would be to buy plastic sheets, available at most quilt shops or art supply shops. The beauty of plastic is that it doesn't wear out and only one is needed for each quilt.

How to Make a Quilt

1. Make templates for each pattern piece. If using cardboard, make several since the cardboard will wear down from tracing around it. A heavy-gauge plastic is also available at quilt and craft stores for this purpose.

2. Lay templates on fabric, having the grainline run straight on at least two sides. Trace and cut out.

3. Piece the top, following instructions.

4. When the top is completed, mark it for quilting. Use a #2 or #3 lead pencil for light fabrics, or a dressmaker's white pencil for dark fabrics. If you are using one of the synthetic quilt batts, lines can be about 1″ apart. For cotton batts, lines should be closer.

5. Spread the top out flat, right side facing down. Spread the batt on the top, then add the backing fabric. Baste the three layers together. If you are going to machine-quilt, you might want to anchor the three layers with long pins or safety pins.

6. Using a small running stitch, quilt along the lines you have marked.

7. Cut bias strips 2″ wide to fit along each side of the quilt. Stitch in place to the front of the quilt. Flip the raw edge over to the back, turn under and stitch.

Equipment and Supplies

You probably have on hand most of the supplies needed to make every project in this book. Even a sewing machine isn't absolutely necessary although it does make the work faster and easier.

You will need:

Rulers: 12″ and 18″ are nice to have, especially the two-inch-wide see-through rulers with markings every quarter inch.

Pencils

Scissors

Needles: regular sewing needles and crochet hooks as specified

Pins

Sewing thread: button and carpet thread and twine for lacing.

Rotary cutter (very nice to have): There is a special ruler available for use with the rotary cutter. It measures 6″ × 24″ and is marked every quarter inch, both crosswise and lengthwise. If you don't want to invest in that, you can make one from a ¼″ to ½″ thick piece of plexiglass. Cut the Plexiglass 24″ to 36″ long, and 6″ wide, making sure that the edge is straight and true. Measure the Plexiglass every inch and place a strip of masking tape across it. This works fine for strips that are an even inch.

Sunday in the Park

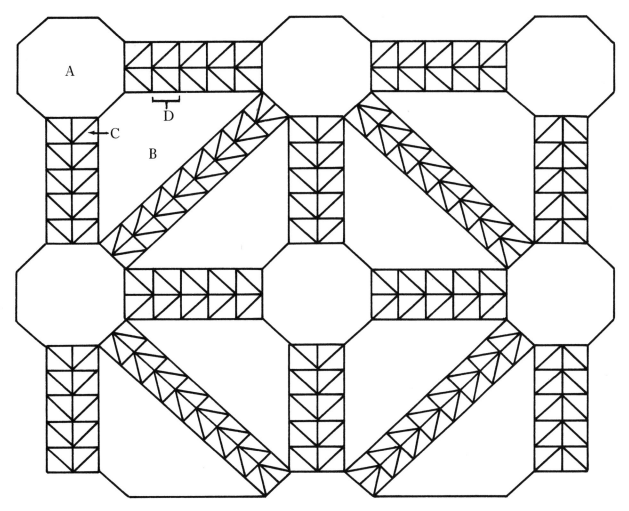

Setting diagram

Quilt size: 90″ × 90″
Pieces per quilt:
  A 25 yellow
  B 32 green
  C 688 white
    688 scrap prints

This is a difficult pattern to piece because part A is set in and each corner must be exact. When making templates A and B, include seam allowance. Then draw around the pattern within the seam allowance, and make a small hole at the seam of each corner. Mark this point onto the fabric. *It is extremely important that no stitches extend beyond this mark.* Part C does not need to

be marked at each corner, but the corners should be marked once the strips are assembled so they can be matched to the marks on the fabric of A and B.

A word of explanation about part C. I'm sure you recognize the *Flying Geese* pattern and may wonder why I used two squares made of triangles rather than a large triangle and two small ones. First, I find it faster and get a better match by joining the two squares. You can feed the two triangles through the machine in a long strip, cut them apart, match to another triangle, and feed these through in no time at all. Second, the smaller pattern piece allows me to take advantage of smaller pieces of fabric.

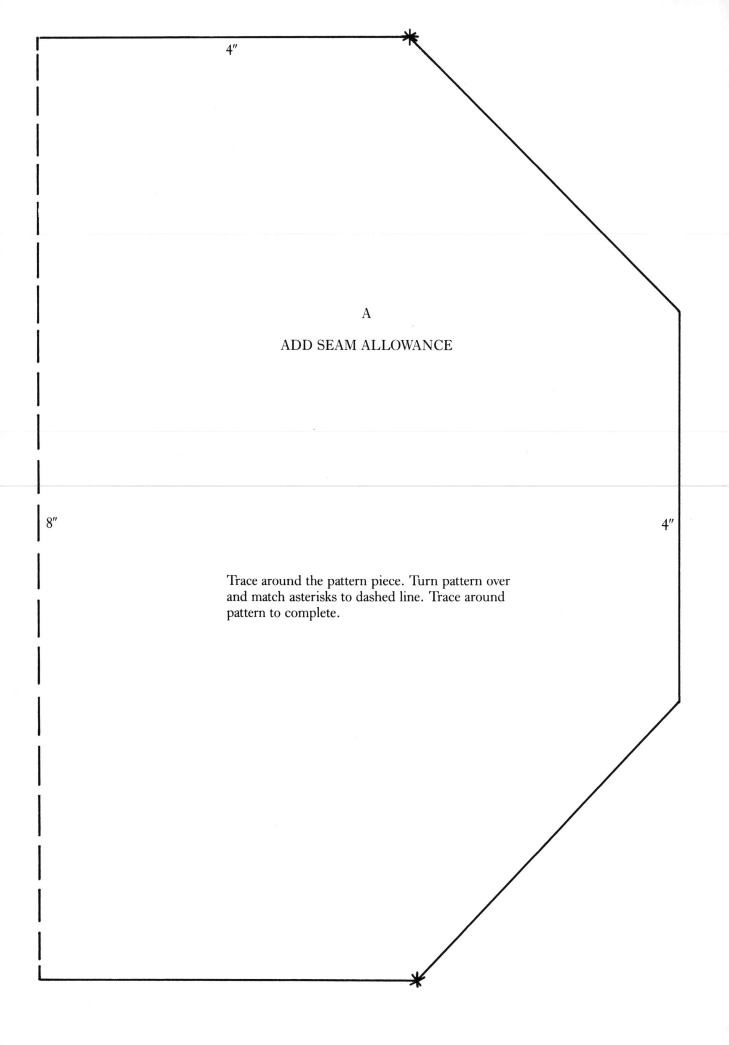

4″

A

ADD SEAM ALLOWANCE

8″

4″

Trace around the pattern piece. Turn pattern over
and match asterisks to dashed line. Trace around
pattern to complete.

4″

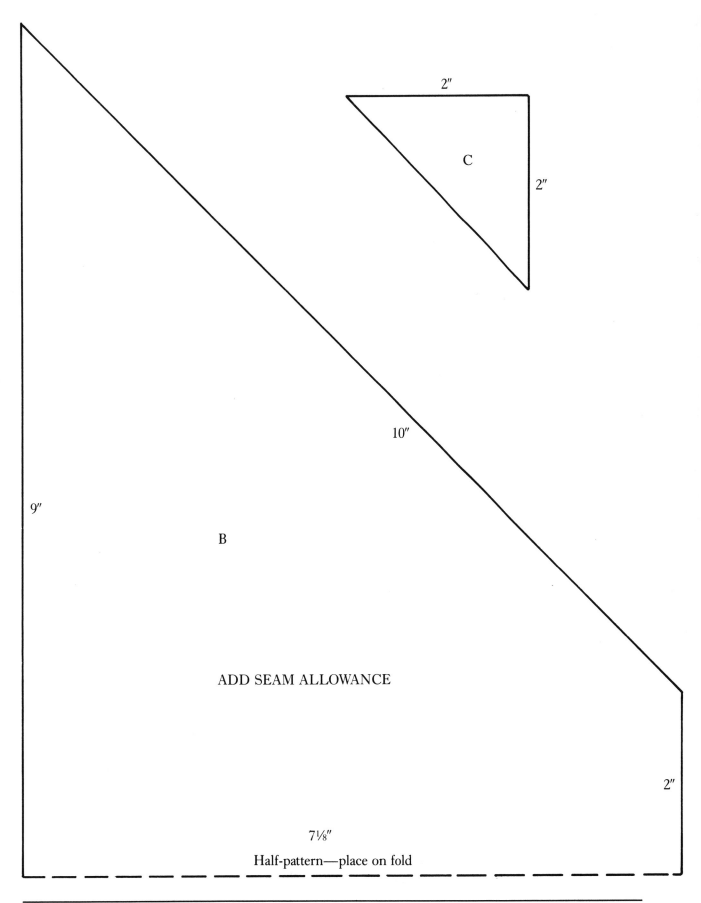

2"

2"

C

10"

9"

B

ADD SEAM ALLOWANCE

2"

7⅛"

Half-pattern—place on fold

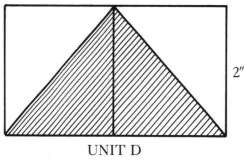

UNIT D

Assembly

Sew one white C to one print C to form a square. Join two identical squares to form unit D.

Join nine unit D's to form a strip. You will need sixteen strips. You will also need forty strips made up of five unit D's.

Beginning in the upper-left corner, follow the diagram for direction of strips. Sew a nine-unit D between two B's. Sew a five-unit D to each straight side. Sew an A to each corner. This is the tricky part. Pin A to B at the corner, being careful to match up the marks. Sew. Then sew an A to one of the five-unit strips, matching the corners. Repeat for the other corners. Again, do not stitch beyond the mark.

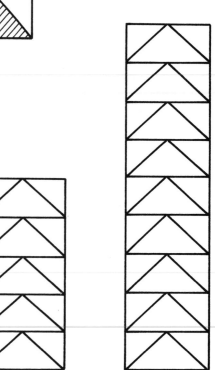

Autumn Tints

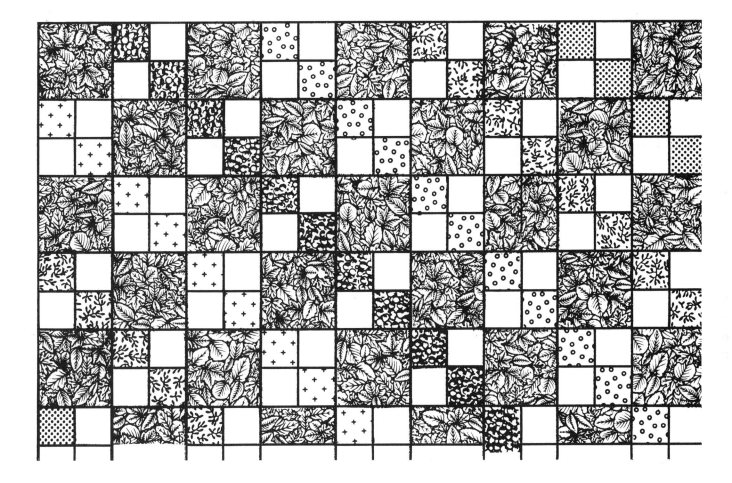

This is a very quick and easy pattern, since it is made up entirely of squares. Denims, corduroys, heavyweight cottons, and even double knits could be used to good advantage for an everyday, tied quilt.

Quilt size: This is easily made to any size desired. Just keep adding rows until you reach the size you want.

Materials: Assorted scraps and enough of one solid color to carry throughout for the four square patches.

Study the diagram of the quilt and plan how you will use your scraps. Cut templates and fabric. Sew the four-patch squares (B), then join to the large squares (A) in rows.

For the border, I sewed strips of $2'' \times 6''$ rectangles, using the same fabrics as those in the quilt top.

A

B

ADD SEAM ALLOWANCE

Sawtooth

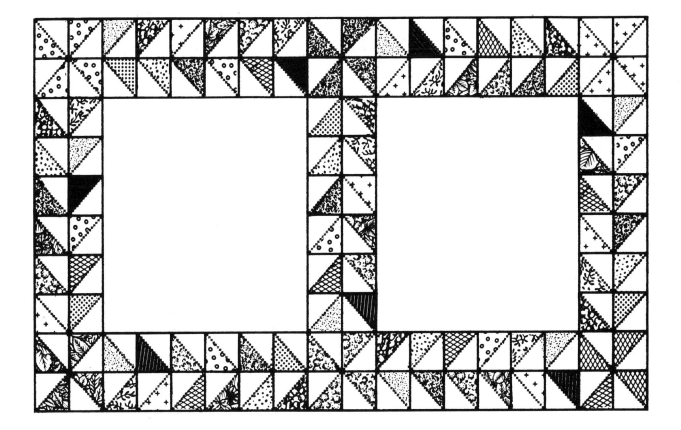

This quilt is easy but it does take a long time to finish. When I made it, I used white and print triangles to form the little 2″ squares, but it might be more interesting to use a light-colored print with a dark print.

Make the template for the half-square triangles (you will need several if using cardboard) and cut out the pieces. Assemble into squares. At the intersection of each block, a pinwheel is formed, so make sure that these are the same color.

The number of 12″ squares needed will depend on the size of quilt you want.

My quilt measures 84″ × 100″ and requires thirty 12″ squares.

Assembly

If making the same size quilt, you will need six pinwheel squares for each row. Adjust the number if your quilt is smaller.

Join the squares into strips as shown in the diagram. Join two strips together.

Starting at the upper left-hand corner, sew together a pinwheel square, a strip of squares, then another pinwheel. Continue until the desired width is reached.

For the second row, turn a strip so it runs vertically, join to a 12″ square, continue alternating across. Join to the first row. Keep adding rows until the desired size is reached.

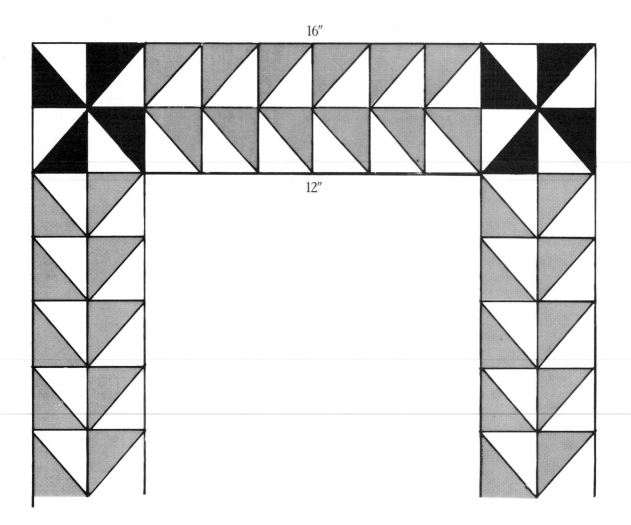

16"

12"

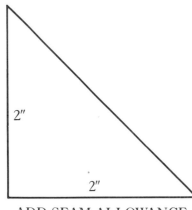

2"

2"

ADD SEAM ALLOWANCE

Braid and Stripe

This is another fairly easy pattern and your only difficulty may be in starting the braid strip. Just remember that the beginning of the strip is cut off so that it is even.

Make a template of the pattern and cut out fabric, remembering to reverse half the pieces.

Another way to do this is to discard the pattern piece and use the rectangle. You don't have to reverse the pattern, just cut them all the same. Sew together in the same way and when the strip is finished, cut off the jagged edges.

Decide how long you want the quilt to be and make your braid strip that length. Cut strips from a complementary fabric of the same length and join together, alternating, until the quilt is the desired width. Remember to start and end with the same strip.

The width of the plain strip can be equal to the braid strip, wider or narrower.

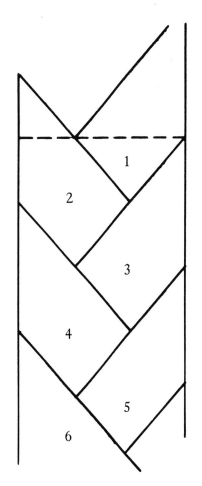

The diagram shows the sequence of sewing the patches together

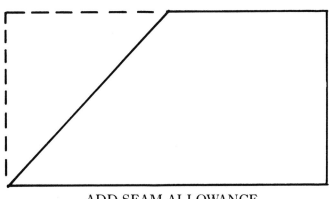

ADD SEAM ALLOWANCE

This and That

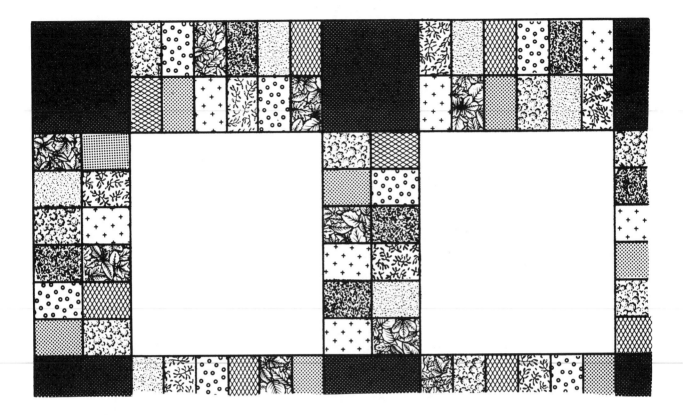

This is an easy pattern to piece. The small rectangles can be strip-pieced, then cut apart. The two remaining pieces are simply a 4″ and a 6″ square.

This quilt should use a wide variety of fabrics and for best results, you should have most of the rectangular strips assembled before you begin to set the quilt so that you have an even distribution of the different prints throughout the quilt rather than have clumps of colors and patterns in one area.

To Strip-Piece

Select six pieces of fabric, cutting them about the same length. Cut each length to measure 2″ wide. This allows for a ½″ seam allowance. If you prefer to use a ¼″ seam allowance, cut the strips 1½″ wide. Seam the six strips together to form a "fabric" 7″ wide. Press.

Lay the fabric out on a flat surface. Even off one end if it isn't already. Measure and mask the strip every 2″ (be sure to add seam allowance) and cut apart. Then sew two strips together according to the diagram.

Strip-piecing is the fastest way to sew the rectangles, but don't hesitate to use the template in the usual way to utilize small scraps of fabric.

When you have a good stack of assembled rectangles, you're ready to set the top together.

Cut out the 6″ square from white fabric. I used blue throughout for the 4″ square, but you could also use scraps for this piece, too.

Assembly

The quilt is set in strips, beginning at the top. Start with a blue square, add a rectangle strip, then a square. Continue across to the desired width.

The second row begins with a rectangle strip

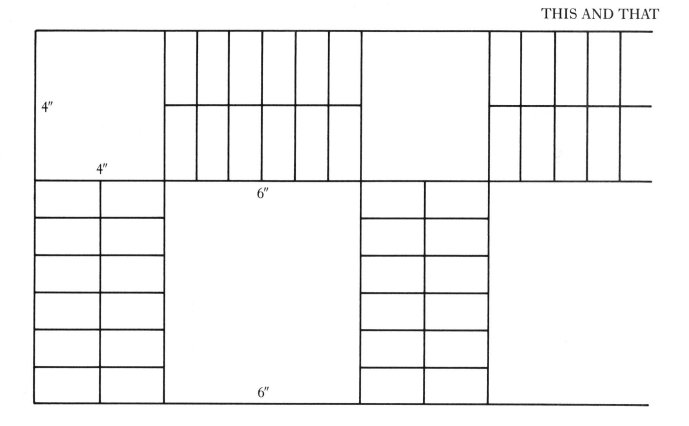

4″

4″

6″

6″

set up and down, then a white square, then another strip, across the quilt. Then sew the rows together. Continue in this way until the quilt is the desired size. Be sure to end with a blue square and rectangle strip the same as you started to form a border.

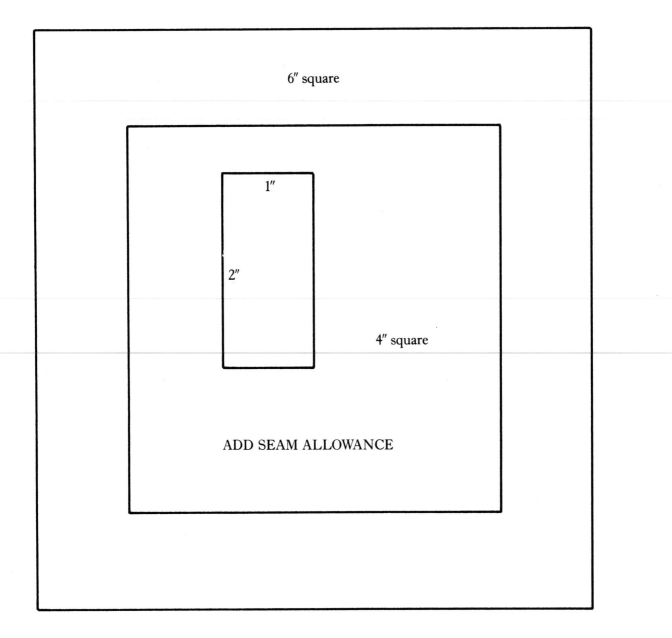

6″ square

1″

2″

4″ square

ADD SEAM ALLOWANCE

Endless Chain

Block size: 8″ × 9″ (4½″-sided hexagon)

Only three pattern pieces are needed to create this interesting design, and it will use up a lot of oddly shaped scraps.

Six each of A and B are sewn alternately to form a hexagon, and a circle (C) is added for the center. You can either zigzag-stitch it in place, or whipstitch it down as you would in appliqué. To form a perfect circle, add seam allowance to pattern and cut out. Cut out a template of the exact size circle. Run a gathering stitch around the outer edge of the circle, lay the template on the circle and pull up the thread. Press.

When joining the blocks, be sure not to stitch beyond the seam line. This will avoid problems and puckers since adjoining rows are set into each other.

Jack's Chain

There are several versions of this design, each with a different name. *Friendship Chain* and *Rosalia's Flower Garden* are two of them.

Friendship Chain uses a small rectangle, 1″ × 1½″; *Jack's Chain* uses a larger rectangle, measuring 1″ × 3″. *Rosalia's Flower Garden* divides this larger rectangle into a 9-patch block of 1″ squares.

Assembly

Make the units that go around the hexagon according to the diagrams. You can take advantage of small pieces by cutting each square or rectangle individually, or, if you have some strips, strip-piece the units, then cut apart.

Sew a completed unit to each side of the hexagon, then set in the triangle. *Be sure not to stitch beyond the seam line.* This completes the first block. For the second and succeeding blocks, sew a hexagon to a strip unit, then sew more units around the second hexagon, filling in the triangle pieces as needed.

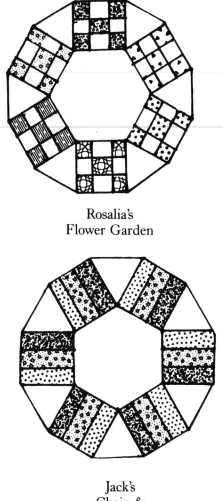

Rosalia's
Flower Garden

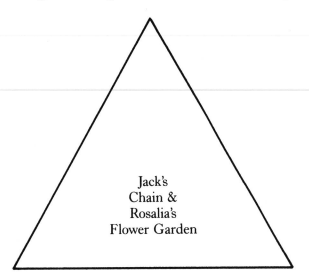

Jack's
Chain &
Rosalia's
Flower Garden

Jack's Chain

Jack's
Chain &
Friendship
Chain

ADD SEAM ALLOWANCE

All three designs are assembled the same way. Friendship Chain uses the smaller triangle; Jack's Chain and Rosalia's Flower Garden use the large triangle.

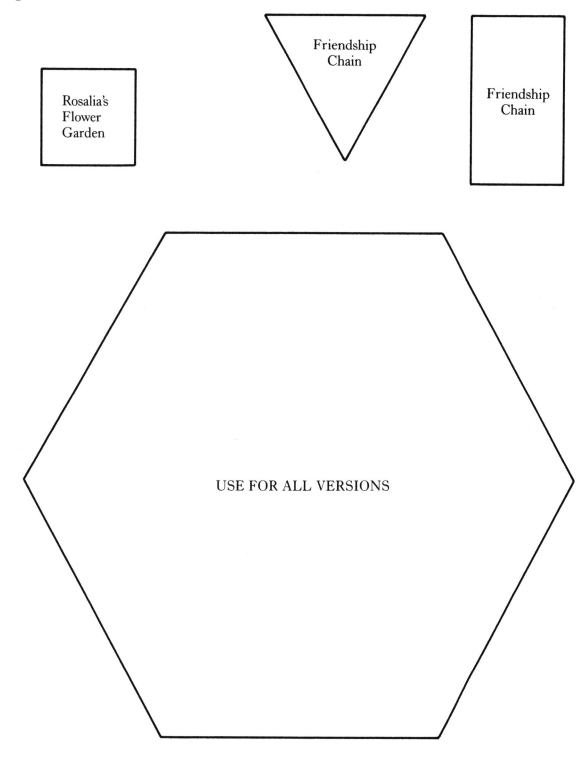

Rosalia's Flower Garden

Friendship Chain

Friendship Chain

USE FOR ALL VERSIONS

Nine-Patch Scrap

Block size: 12"
Quilt size: 36" × 48"
This is another design that can be strip-pieced, cut apart and sewn back together in the proper order.

To Strip-Piece

Cut three fabrics into 2"-wide strips. Sew together, using a ½" seam allowance. Press. Measure the strip every four inches and cut apart. You now have a 4" × 4" square. Sew these squares together, alternating the direction of the strips as shown in the diagram. Add the corner triangles to complete the block.

Small pieces of fabric can be sewn using a template 1" × 3". Add seam allowance when cutting.

This quilt required twelve blocks, but you can make it to any size just by adding more rows of blocks.

1" × 3"

ADD SEAM ALLOWANCE

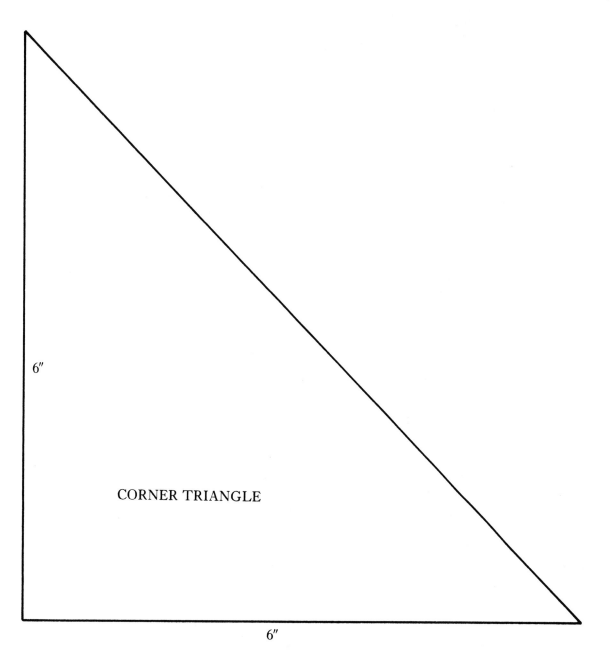

6″

CORNER TRIANGLE

6″

ADD SEAM ALLOWANCE

Improved Nine-Patch

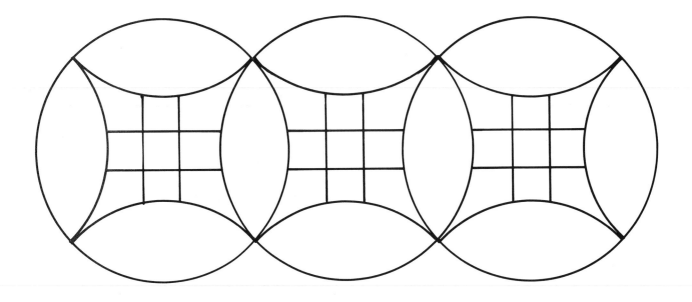

This pattern makes a lovely scrap quilt, and the curves are gentle enough so that the sewing is not too difficult. The block is assembled just like a regular nine-patch. I've included two sizes; the small one lets you use up lots of tiny pieces, while the larger one lets you get the quilt finished faster.

Of course, my strip-piecing method makes either size go together quickly.

Select two contrasting fabrics. For the smaller version, cut two strips from each fabric 3½″ wide and one strip from each fabric measuring 2¼″ wide. Seam the strips together, the two wide ones with the narrower contrasting one in the center.

Lay template A on the strip and trace around. Allow for seam allowances, and trace around B, then A again. This sequence makes one block. Repeat marking in sequence the length of the strip and on the second strip. Cut out and seam contrasting width strips together. The two strips will make about 10 blocks.

The larger pattern can also be strip pieced. Make a pattern by tracing around A, lay B up against the line of A and trace around, then A again. The fabric strips should measure 4¾″ and 3″ wide.

Set blocks together with part C.

If you have difficulty joining the units so they match exactly, you might want to try my set and quilt method also.

Mark the fabric units on the right side. Lay out sixteen of the assembled nine-patch units in the order you want them in the quilt. This is a nice size for easy manipulation on the sewing machine. Cut a piece of backing fabric a little larger than the blocks as set together. Lay batting on top.

Position the blocks on the batting, matching points, and pin in place. Turn under the seam

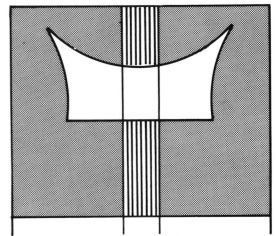

Layout for strip-piecing

allowance on the D piece and pin in place between the blocks, matching the curves on each side. Stitch in place. The stitching also serves as the quilting. Quilt along the seams of the 9-patch units and add a few quilting lines to the D pieces. Keep making blocks and joining to the previous ones until the quilt is the size you want it to be. Add binding and the quilt is finished.

If strip-piecing, use templates as given. If hand-piecing, cut templates apart.

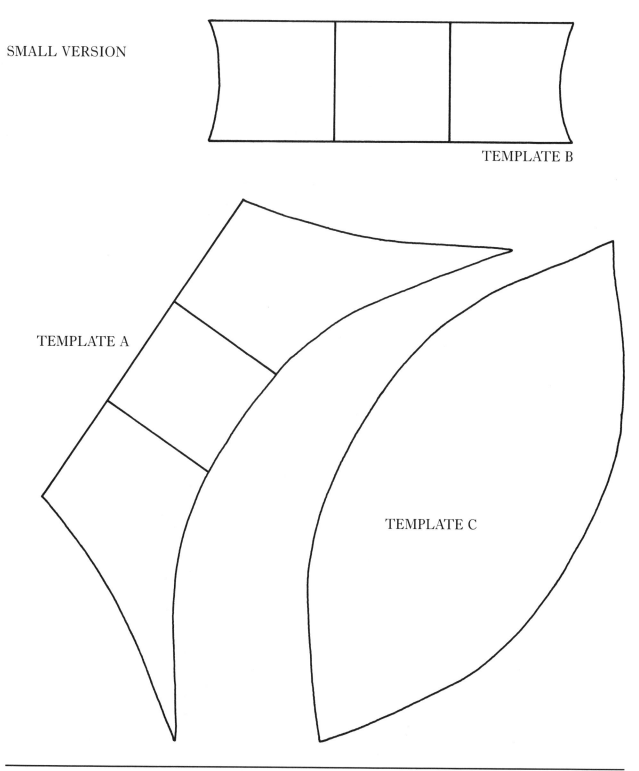

SMALL VERSION

TEMPLATE B

TEMPLATE A

TEMPLATE C

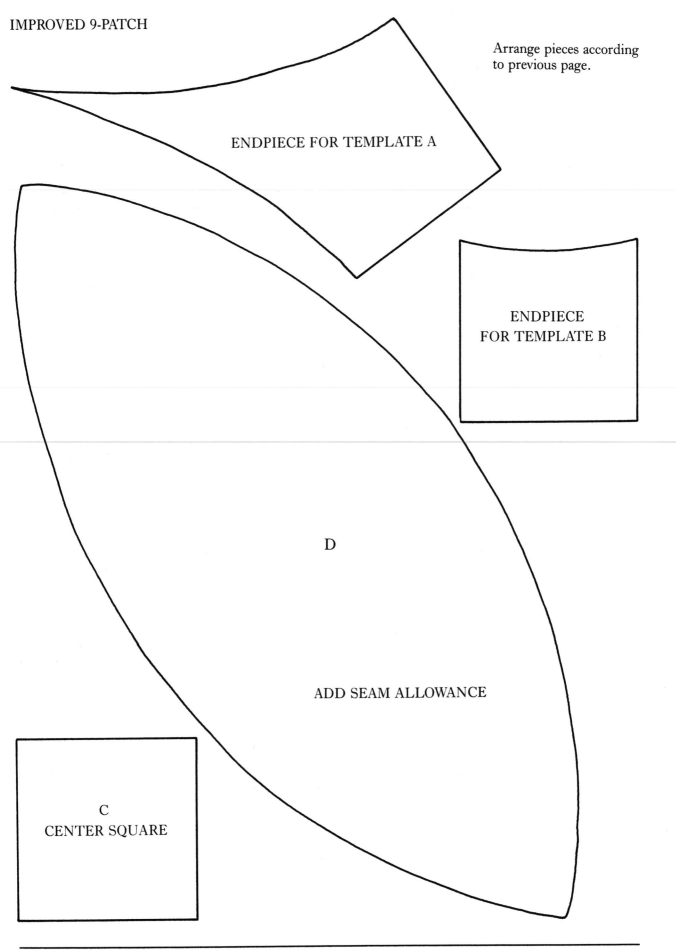

IMPROVED 9-PATCH

Arrange pieces according
to previous page.

ENDPIECE FOR TEMPLATE A

ENDPIECE
FOR TEMPLATE B

D

ADD SEAM ALLOWANCE

C
CENTER SQUARE

Multiple Squares

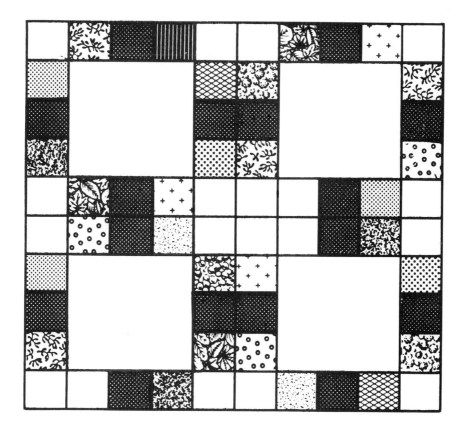

This pattern is so easy that it hardly needs instructions. Piece three small squares, following the placement as shown, into a strip and attach to top and bottom of the plain square. Make two strips of five squares each and attach to sides. There's your 10″ block.

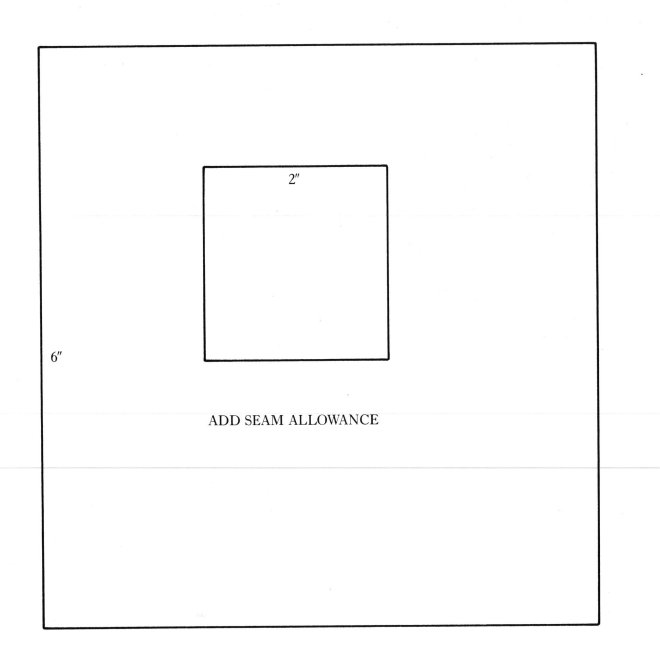

2″

6″

ADD SEAM ALLOWANCE

Above: Three wreaths in different sizes and made with different techniques. At top is the Prairie Point, page 88. Right is a Bow Tie wreath, page 90; at bottom is a Yo-Yo wreath, page 89. All are quick and easy to make. Right: Ocean Waves quilt, page 43.

A

Above: a backgammon board, page 96, the other side is a checkerboard; Fire Screen, page 122; and at bottom a Daisy potholder, page 101.

Right: Amish Pinwheels, page 46.

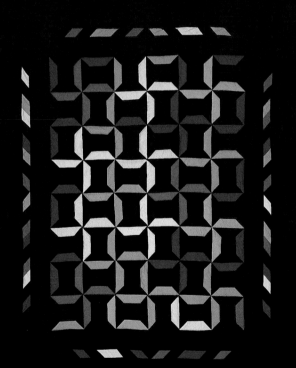

At the center of this all-Christmas page is a Tabletop Tree, page 70. At top is a Six-Point Star, page 79; a Yo-Yo ornament, page 80; a Fan ornament, page 78; Mitten ornaments, page 81; and a Sleepy Santa Claus, page 72. At left is a Dresden Plate Tree Skirt, page 86. C

A group of useful gifts: a Padded Hanger, page 107; a Gay 90's Stocking, page 82, which can be used after Christmas as a lingerie bag; a Garment Cover, page 108; and a Rose Trellis Appliqué Screen, page 119.

D

The Chair Caddy above, page 109, will fit almost any chair. The two place mats are a Cookie Cutter place mat, page 63, and a Tall Pine Tree place mat, page 66.

At left is a version of the Sawtooth quilt, page 17.

E

Two unusual ideas for a small quilt:
an Exercise Mat, page 104, which
in these days of the home workout is
almost an essential. Having made
one exercise mat, why not a second,
which can be combined with the first
to make a Sleeping Bag, page 105?

Above is side one of your sleeping bag,
which is called Under the Stars. At
right is side two, Moon over the City.

F

At top is a Beach Blanket Tote, page 115, a practical luxury. The bottom quilt is April's Valentine, page 99, which was designed by the author's daughter at the age of eight, and which might be an excellent design to teach a small child the art of quilting.

Clockwise: a Wall Basket, page 110, excellent for a dried floral arrangement; a Cup potholder, page 102, which could also be used as a coaster for a hot drink; a Flower potholder, page 103; and a Chalet appliance cover, page 94.

H

Thrifty Wife

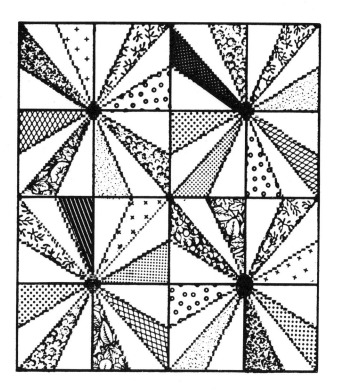

This unique design is not really difficult to piece. The simplest way is to assemble each quarter of the 10″ block, then join the four quarters. Appliqué the circle in the center.

This is a good design to play with for different effects. If you make a line drawing, you'll see many possibilities that aren't readily apparent with the colors in place.

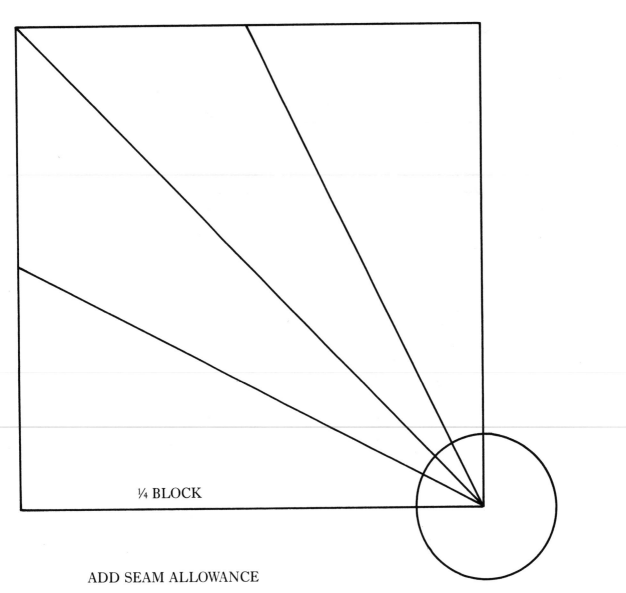

¼ BLOCK

ADD SEAM ALLOWANCE

Odd-Scraps Patchwork

Block: 10″
This is another super-easy pattern. Just follow
the diagram for placement of the patches.

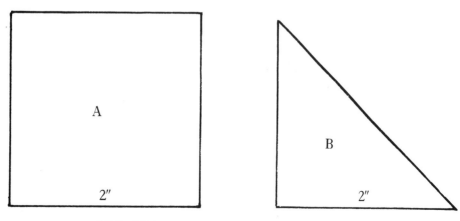

ADD SEAM ALLOWANCE

String Star

This is a super-easy design that makes a big impact.

Your first step is to make a foundation fabric. Select all sorts of colors and patterns in strips ranging from 1″ to 3″ wide. Sew these strips together to form a fabric, with the stripes going across the fabric. Lay pattern piece A on this fabric and cut out. Each block requires four A and four white B pieces.

Assembly

Sew together four A-B units. Join two of these units to make half the block. Join two such units to complete. Completed blocks are joined side by side until the desired size is reached.

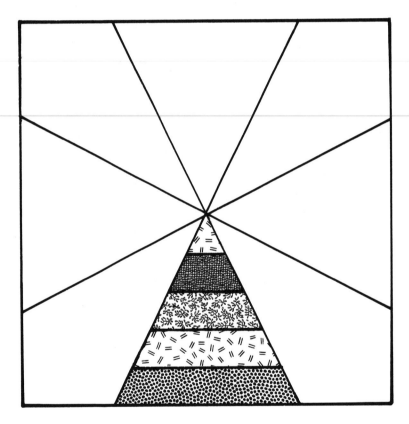

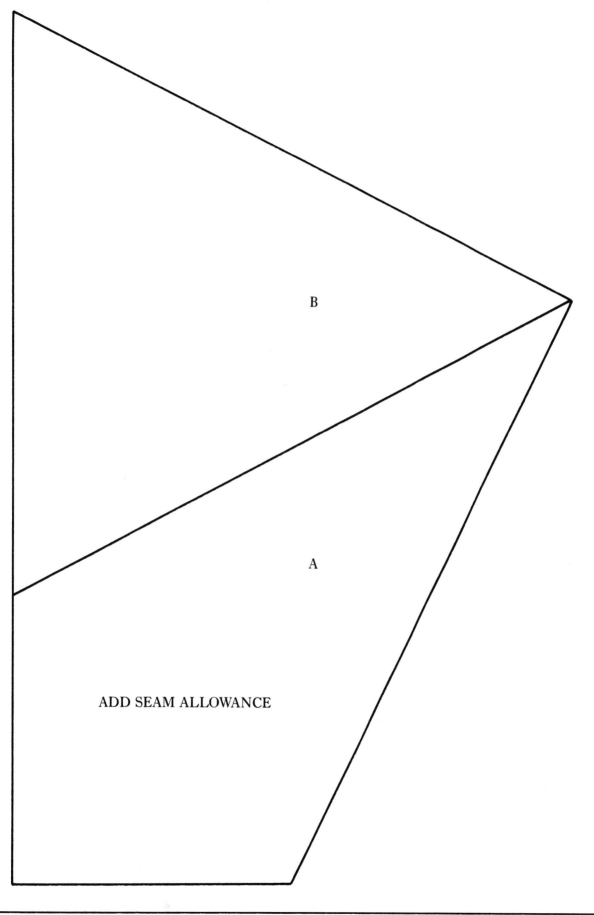

B

A

ADD SEAM ALLOWANCE

May Basket

This 10″ block should be set with alternate plain blocks. Add seam allowance and make template for plain blocks. When all the full blocks have been cut, cut the template in half to form a triangle. Add seam allowance to cut edge. This fills in along the outside edges.

For the corners, cut the template in half again, and add seam allowance to the cut edge. Cut four corner triangles.

To assemble the block, follow the diagrams.

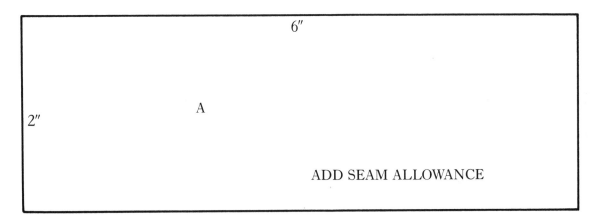

6″

2″

A

ADD SEAM ALLOWANCE

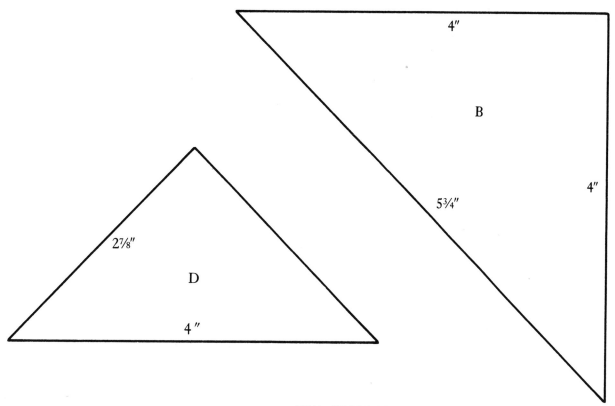

4″

B

5¾″

4″

2⅞″

D

4 ″

ADD SEAM ALLOWANCE

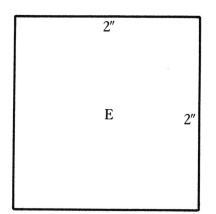

2″

E

2″

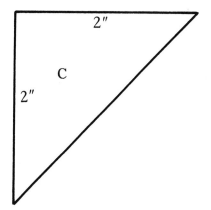

2″

C

2″

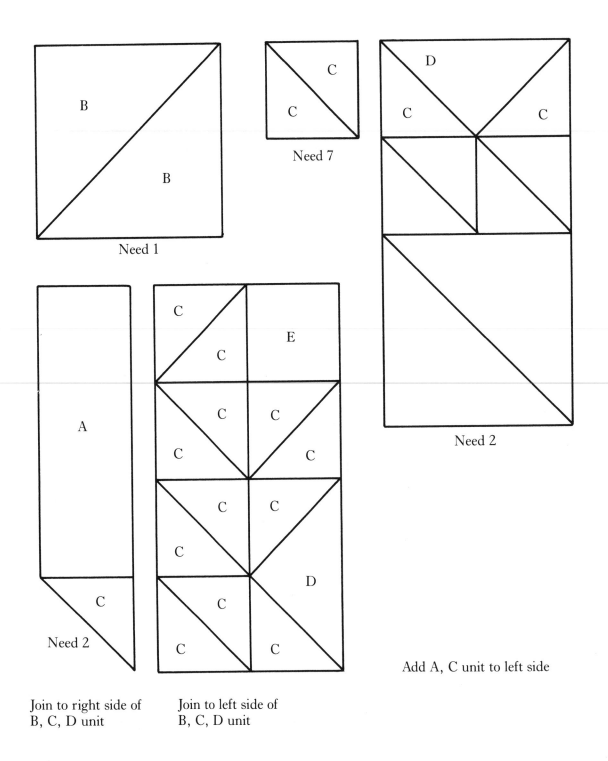

B
B
Need 1

C
C
Need 7

D
C
C
Need 2

A
C
Need 2

C
C
E
C
C
C
C
C
C
C
D
C
C
C
C

Join to right side of
B, C, D unit

Join to left side of
B, C, D unit

Add A, C unit to left side

Complete block by sewing B unit to complete
corner

Missouri Wonder

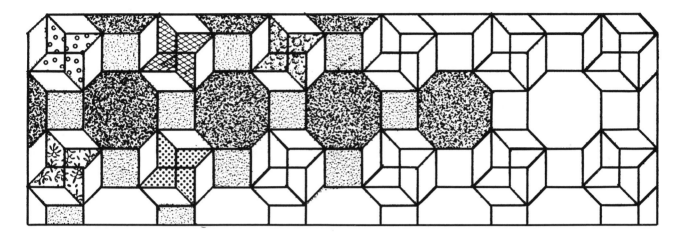

The illustrations show two ways to set the quilt.

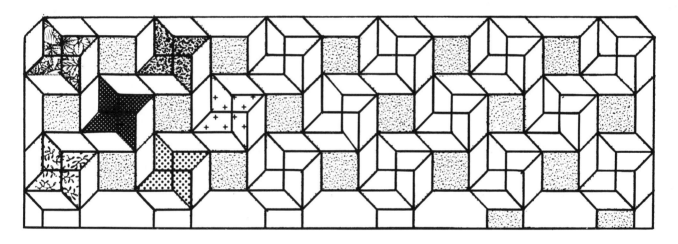

This quilt is fairly easy and fast to put together, if you make sure you do not sew beyond the seam line at the points of the diamonds.

Setting the pieced blocks seven across by seven down will make a quilt 87″ × 87″.

3 yards fabric for the large octagons
2 yards for the squares

Assembly

Sew two sets of A together, then join in the center to form the star. Add the diamonds between the points.

Starting with a pieced block, sew a small square to one side, add the second pieced block. Continue across ending with a pieced block.

The second row starts with a square, then a solid octagon, alternating across the quilt.

For the edges of the quilt, cut the octagon pattern as shown by the dotted line. Set these along the outer edges to form a straight edge.

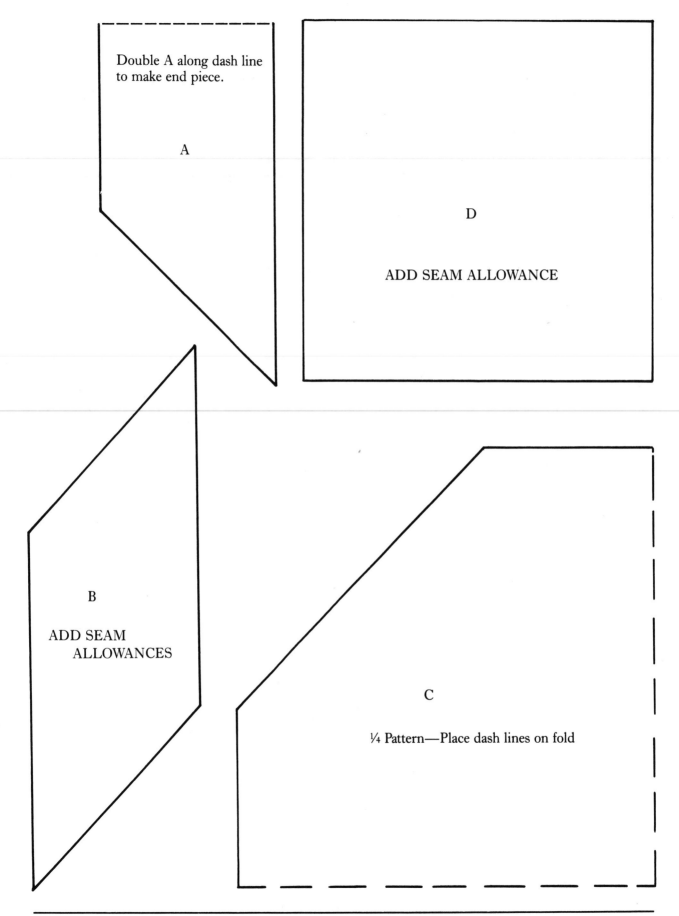

Double A along dash line to make end piece.

A

D

ADD SEAM ALLOWANCE

B

ADD SEAM ALLOWANCES

C

¼ Pattern—Place dash lines on fold

Ocean Waves

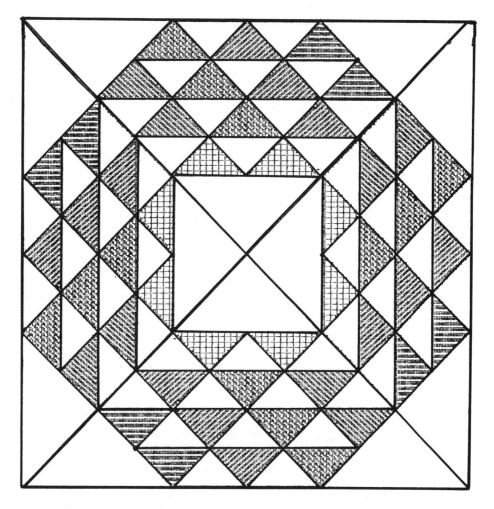

This intricate looking design is really quite easy to piece, and uses up lots and lots of those 2″ triangles. It can be seen in the Color Section.

BLOCK SIZE: 20″

If set four blocks wide by four blocks long, you will have a quilt measuring 80″ × 80″. When I complete the quilt, I intend to add a 3″ or 4″ border in the pink color.

2½ yards solid color fabric

Unit Diagram
4 per block

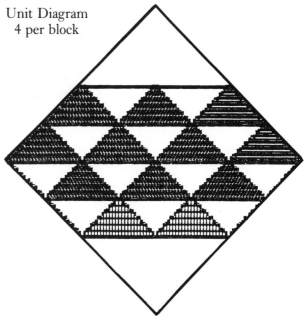

ASSEMBLY

Each block is made up of four sections. Seam together a light and dark triangle to form a square. Each section contains 10 squares, plus four triangles. I used yellow for these triangles throughout the quilt, but you can use an assortment of different colors. Join the triangles as shown in the illustration.

Cut out the 4″ triangles from a solid color fabric and sew to each side of the completed piece to form a square. See illustration.

Join four sections together to form the block, sew in rows to complete the quilt.

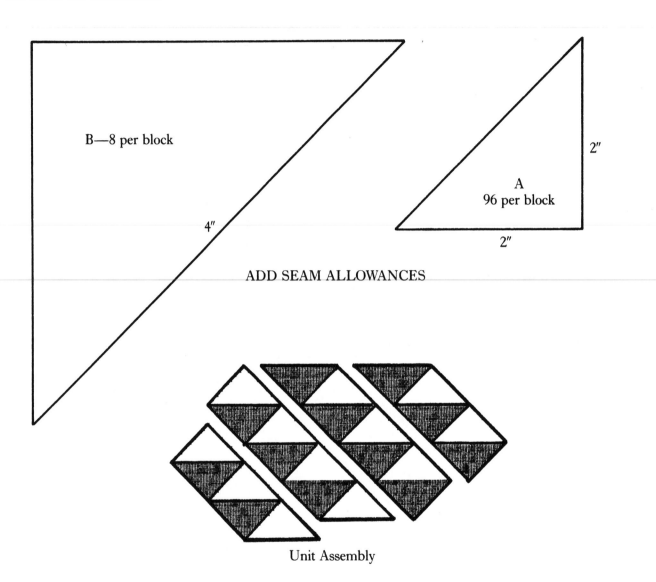

B—8 per block

4″

A
96 per block

2″

2″

ADD SEAM ALLOWANCES

Unit Assembly

Double Pyramids

Here's another pattern for little triangles. This is a large block, measuring 24″, so it won't take many to make a full-size quilt. It is one of the patterns used in making the Tabletop Tree.

Although I used white throughout for the small triangles, it can be made in light and dark colors.

There are six pieced and three plain squares per block. For the pieced squares, sew together six dark and three light triangles to form a square. Arrange them, adding a triangle to the end of each strip. Add the large plain triangle to complete the square. Sew the squares together to form the block.

Because of space limitations, it was necessary to reduce the pattern by 15%.

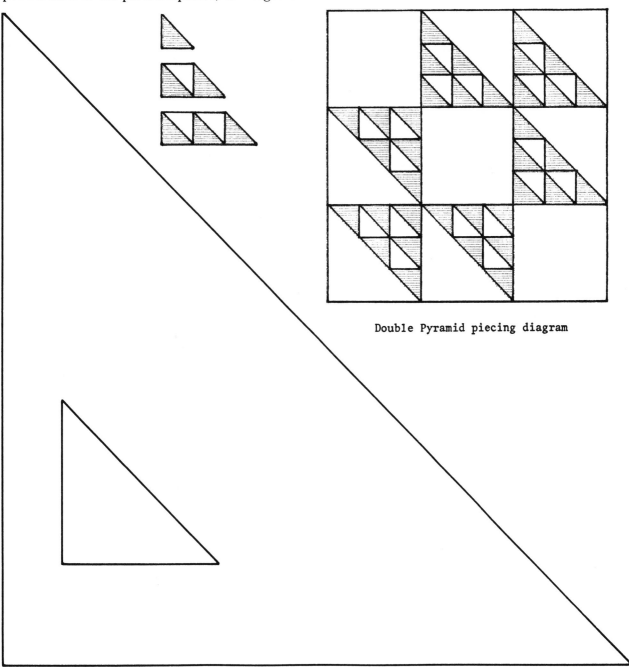

Double Pyramid piecing diagram

Amish Pinwheels

This striking quilt, shown in color on page B of the color section, is a variation on an old favorite, *Spools*. Easy as it is in its original form, by using the strip-piecing method given here, you could have your quilt top completed in one day.

Your first step should be to make a drawing of the top, placing the colors in their proper position. Once you start sewing them together, it can be a little confusing as to which color goes where.

Materials

4 yards black or navy blue
¼ yard each of several bright, solid colors

Using the rotary cutter, measure and cut solid fabrics into 3″ wide strips across the grain.

To best utilize the fabric, sew a colored strip to each edge of a 3″ black strip. A complete pinwheel requires four blocks of each color. Press.

Make a template of the triangle, being sure to mark the line shown. Lay the template on the sewn fabric strips, lining up the line on the template with the seam line. Alternate from side to side when cutting triangles.

Cut two black triangles to each 8″ block. Sew the triangles together as shown. Sew four completed blocks together, matching your plan for color placement.

Quilt layout example with six blocks assembled

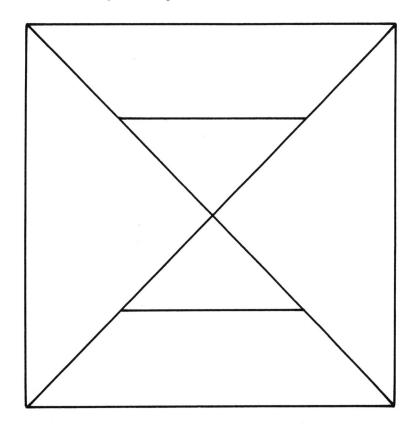

On the pieced strip, lay the center line of the pattern on the seam line.

The entire pattern is used to cut the solid triangles.

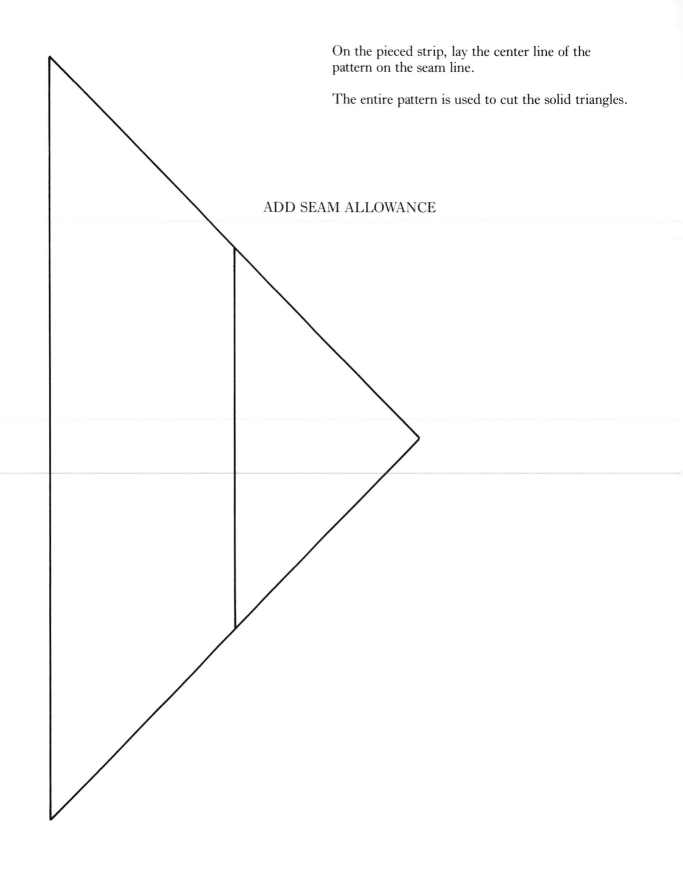

ADD SEAM ALLOWANCE

Diamonds and Squares

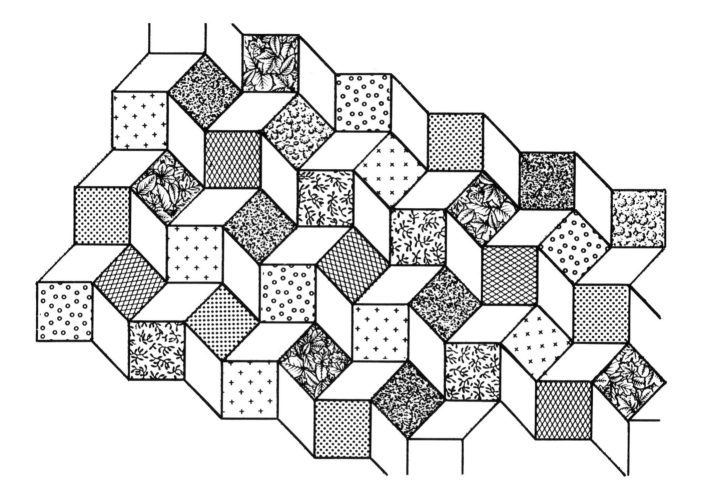

I assembled this design on the sewing machine and encountered no problems at all. The secret is accurate marking of the fabric.

In this instance, I used a ¼″ seam allowance, cutting the squares to measure 3″. I did not mark the sewing line on the squares, but you can if it makes it easier for you. The diamonds were marked with both the sewing line and the cutting line.

Begin at the upper left-hand side with a square. Sew a diamond to it, then alternate squares and diamonds across the row for 18 squares. The second row begins with a diamond, alternating with seventeen squares.

To sew the rows together, I found it easier to sew one diamond/square at a time. Since I marked only the diamonds, I began with the diamond up so that I could see the sewing line. Align it with the square in the upper row, sew this square together, and cut the thread. Be sure to leave the seam allowances free. Turn it over and do the next pair. Continue in this way across the row. It really doesn't take as long as it might sound, and it's a lot easier than trying to pivot for the zigzag shape of the rows.

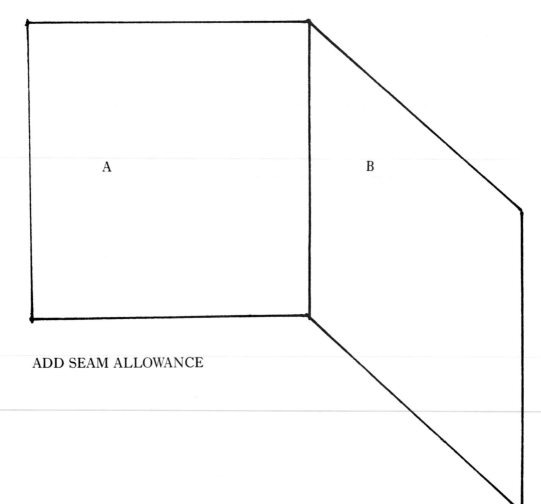

A

B

ADD SEAM ALLOWANCE

Brilliant Star

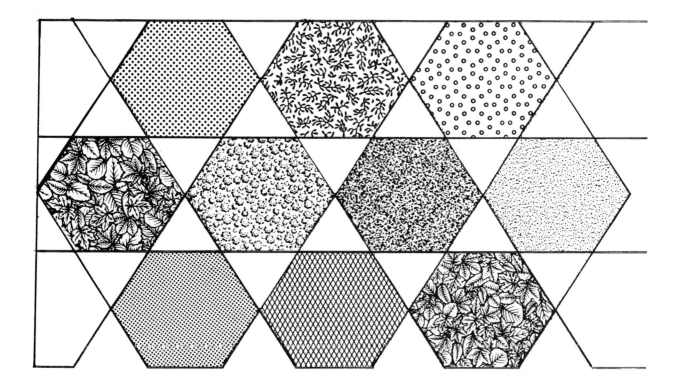

This is another quilt that is easy to do if you remember not to sew beyond the seam line.

There are only two pattern pieces, and the quilt is assembled in rows.

Place the hexagon so that the flat side is top and bottom. Beginning at the top left-hand side of the quilt, sew a triangle to each face of the left-hand side, and one triangle to the upper right side.

Select the second hexagon and sew a triangle to the lower left side. Pin the two hexagons together, matching seam lines and edges, and stitch. Continue across for fifteen hexagons, which makes the quilt 84″ wide. Row 2 begins with a hexagon without the triangles on the outer edge. Each row measures 4½″ deep, so it will take 20 rows to equal 90″.

PIECING DIAGRAM

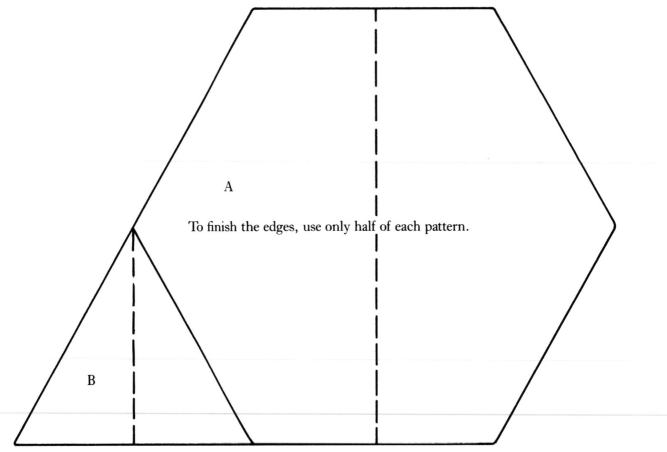

A

To finish the edges, use only half of each pattern.

B

ADD SEAM ALLOWANCE

AN ASSORTMENT OF POSSIBILITIES

Pieced quilt patterns, being geometric in nature, are easily adapted to many projects simply by scaling them up or down in size. Regardless of whether you're scaling up or down, the method is the same.

First, decide what size you want the pattern to be, then select a pattern that can be scaled to that size. If you want a finished block to be 3″, select a nine-patch pattern. This is easy to divide into three sections. Later, when you are more confident, you can try some of the designs that will require using fractions.

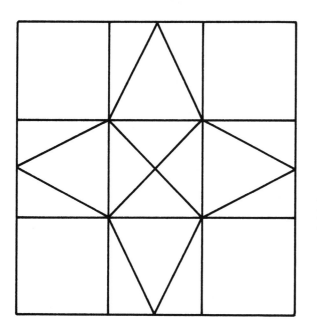

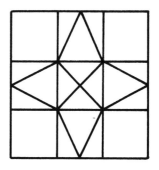

Draw a grid to the desired size and transfer the lines within each square.

SPLIT 9–PATCH

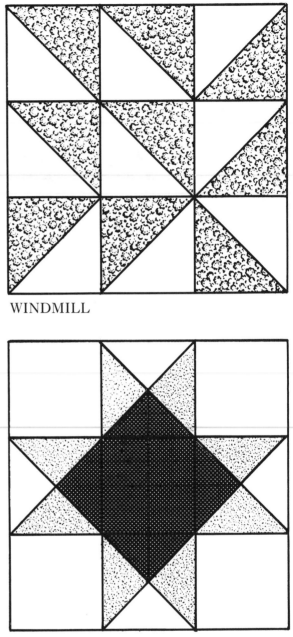

WINDMILL

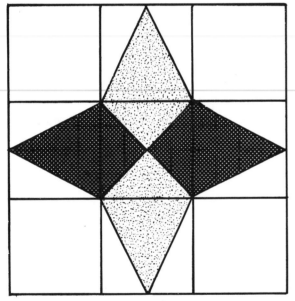

ARKANSAS SNOWFLAKE

VARIABLE STAR

Miniature blocks open up a whole realm of decorative possibilities. There are several projects that use miniature blocks, but in addition to these, try them for clothing trim, pillows, towels, sheets, pillowcases, tablecloths, curtains and of course, quilts, from dollhouse size to a full-scale quilt. I saw a full-size quilt in a museum made entirely of 3″ basket blocks. Can't you just imagine a sampler quilt made from 3″ or 4″ blocks.

To get you started, on the following pages I've included mini blocks ranging in size from 3″ to 6″.

Miniature Quilt Block Place Mats

Materials for Each Place Mat

Backing fabric cut 13″ × 19″
Design fabric for top, cut 15″ × 13″
3 pieced miniature 4″ blocks
1¾ yd. ruffle trim

PINWHEEL

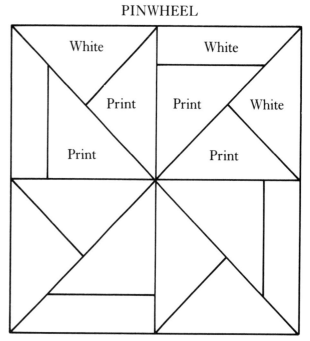

Use a different print for each

BASKET

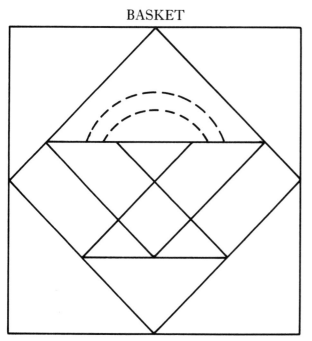

Each block can use different fabrics for the basket

1. Prepare the three miniature blocks and sew together in a strip. Attach the strip to the top fabric (15″ × 13″).
2. Lay pieced front over the backing fabric, wrong sides together. Quilt the two pieces together, leaving the seam allowance free. Turn under the seam allowance and hem. Attach the ruffle trim.

A second method for assembling the backing and top, is to lay them together, right sides facing, and stitch around the edges, leaving an opening for turning. Turn right side out and close the opening; quilt. This method is especially suitable if you are doing the quilting by hand. If machine-quilting, the presser foot may push the fabric, causing creases and folds along the edges.

Too Few Blocks

If you have done much piecework, you probably have an assortment of sample blocks or even a few unfinished quilts. Most of my unfinished quilts came about through lack of proper planning. I started working on a pattern without bothering to see if I had enough fabric to finish it. Several times I didn't, but I have managed to salvage most of these unfinished projects.

If you have your heart set on a quilt, you can first scale down the size of the quilt; instead of a full-size one, make it twin size, or even as a throw for naps on the couch.

A second choice would be to set the blocks with alternate plain blocks or lattice strips. To stretch the blocks even more, set them on the diagonal.

Another alternative is to make up blocks in a harmonizing color scheme and alternate them with what you have.

You can also try different setting arrangements to salvage several blocks that won't quite make a quilt.

In this first example, I had seven blocks I had made many years ago. To make the most of them, I set them on the diagonal, three at the top, three at the bottom and one in the middle. I then filled in with plain white blocks. To relieve some of the white, I filled in the edges with a green polka-dotted fabric that was just slightly different from that used for the leaves in the blocks.

Following are some possible layouts, utilizing varying numbers of blocks.

To use the sample blocks you may have, try a sampler quilt. I've seen some old examples where the blocks were just set side by side, but I think it makes more of an impact, if you set these blocks with lattice strips.

In recent years, the 12″ block seems to have become the standard size for quilt blocks and only occasionally are they scaled larger or smaller. With a little thought in the planning stage, these blocks can be used in your sampler, too.

Use the oversized block as your center block and build around it. Say you have an 18″ block. Add the lattice strips, then flank it with two 8″ or 9″ blocks. Or you could set a 12″ block on the diagonal and fill in the corners. You can add a border to undersized blocks to bring them to the proper size. Just playing with the blocks will give you ideas for their use.

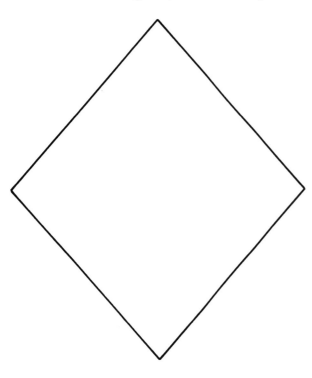

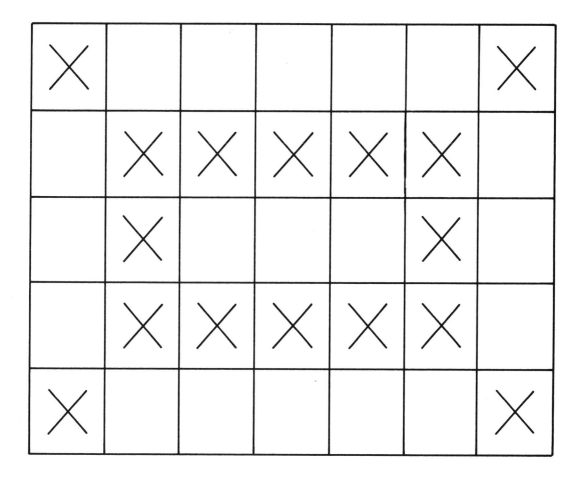

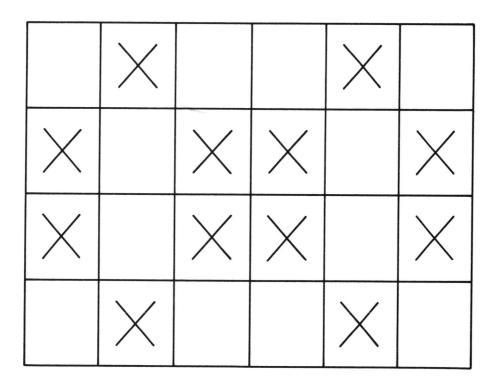

SAMPLE BLOCK SETTINGS

Spider Web Place Mat and Coaster

This is a fast, easy project with tremendous versatility. You should be able to complete a set of four place mats and coasters in an hour or so.

I only used two fabrics for my place mat, but you can use three, four, five or more. The width of each can vary, but the smallest should be at least 1½″ wide to allow for seams.

You could also make the mats reversible by using two patterned blocks and sewing them back to back rather than by finishing the back with a solid color fabric.

1. Make cardboard templates of pattern pieces.
2. Select fabrics and cut into strips. Sew the strips together in the desired order.
3. Lay the template on the completed strip and draw around it, allowing seam allowance between each triangle. For the second triangle, turn the template so that the point faces in the opposite direction as the first one. Alternate the template until you have six triangles.
4. Sew two alternate triangles together, add a third triangle. Repeat with the other three triangles. Join the two halves across the center.

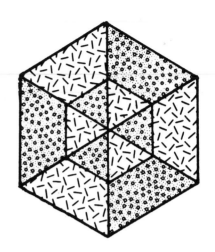

5. Cut out the backing fabric to the same size as the completed *Spider Web*, or make a second block for a reversible mat. Lay the two pieces together, right sides facing, and sew around five sides. Turn the mat right side out and sew the opening closed.

6. Quilt the mat, following your seam lines.

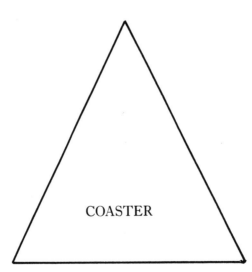

COASTER

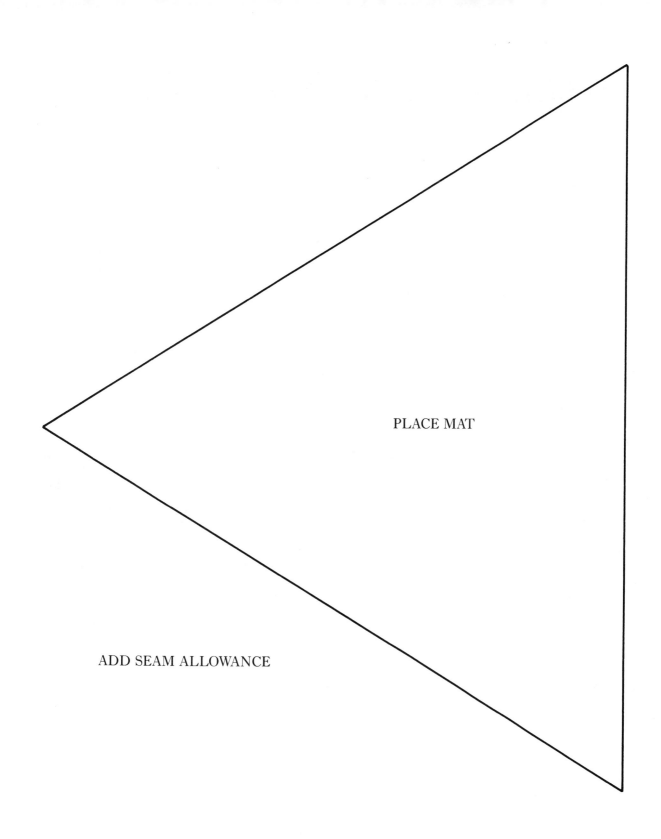

PLACE MAT

ADD SEAM ALLOWANCE

Grandmother's Flower Garden

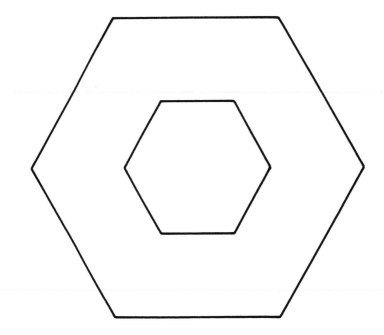

This is very similar to the previous place mat set, but it does take a little longer. I've included two sizes of hexagon. The small one requires six rows to make a place mat, the larger one takes only three.

After you have pieced the block pattern, follow the instructions for the *Spider Web* place mat and coaster on the preceding pages.

Round Tablecloth

This design provides automatic place mats. It does not truly utilize scraps very well since each segment requires a yard square piece of fabric.

The Pattern

Tape sheets of newspaper together to fit the table-top and cut off even with the table edge. Fold the paper circle in quarters to establish the center.

Cut out the hexagon from cardboard, place it in the center and trace around it. Going through the center of the hexagon, draw a straight line from each point to the edge.

At this point, add enough paper to two segments to include the overhang. I made mine 12″ although you can take it to the floor if you wish. Extend the lines forming the segments 12″ or to whatever overhang you've decided on.

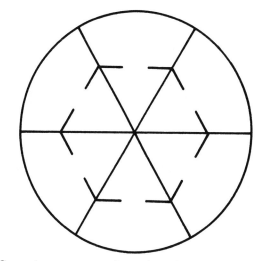

Sew the star together, then insert the wedge shape between the points. Circles have a tendency to cup in the center, so it is a good idea to baste the wedges in place first. Spread it out to see if it lays flat. If not, remove the stitching from one

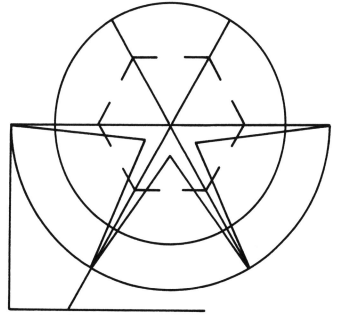

Attach a string to a pen and anchor the loose end to the exact center. Make sure it doesn't move. Place your pen, attached to the string, at the end of one of the extended lines and swing it in an arc to the next extended line.

From the center of the hexagon, measure out 6″ between the lines already drawn and mark. Draw a line from this mark to the line at the outer edge to form the star point.

side of every other segment and spread the seam until it does lay flat. Stitch each segment in place.

I've included a design idea for a square or rectangular table that also provides place mat space. This, of course, has to be scaled up to fit your table. For a square table, use the design once. For a large table, repeat the design as needed.

The standard place-mat size is 12″ × 18″. When looking for patterns to use, consider those that can be adapted to this spacing. *Tick-Tack-Toe* and *Chain Link* are two patterns that can be spread to provide the necessary space. You might also consider some of the border designs to delineate the place-mat spacing.

Cookie Cutter Place Mat

Cookie cutters can be used to make excellent appliqués. Just trace around them on the fabric, add seam allowance and cut out the outline. You can also use them for tree ornaments. Cut out two, sew together and stuff. Trims can be added before or after joining.

Front and lining 13" × 19".

Make patterns of house, road, and gingerbread man and cut from fabric. Cut out five A and four B triangles for tree.

Turn under the raw edges and position all appliqués on background fabric and pin in place before sewing. Wonder Under, a two-sided iron-on material, is excellent to use for turning under the seam allowances. Cut the Wonder Under to the finish size of the appliqué and iron it to the wrong side. Peel off the backing paper. Turn over the seam allowance and press in place. When the appliqué is ready to sew, position it on the fabric and iron in place. Sew the edges of all pieces with a decorative zigzag stitch.

The trees are assembled by turning under the edges of the triangles and stacking them, starting with the small triangle at the top, in a tree shape.

ADD SEAM ALLOWANCE

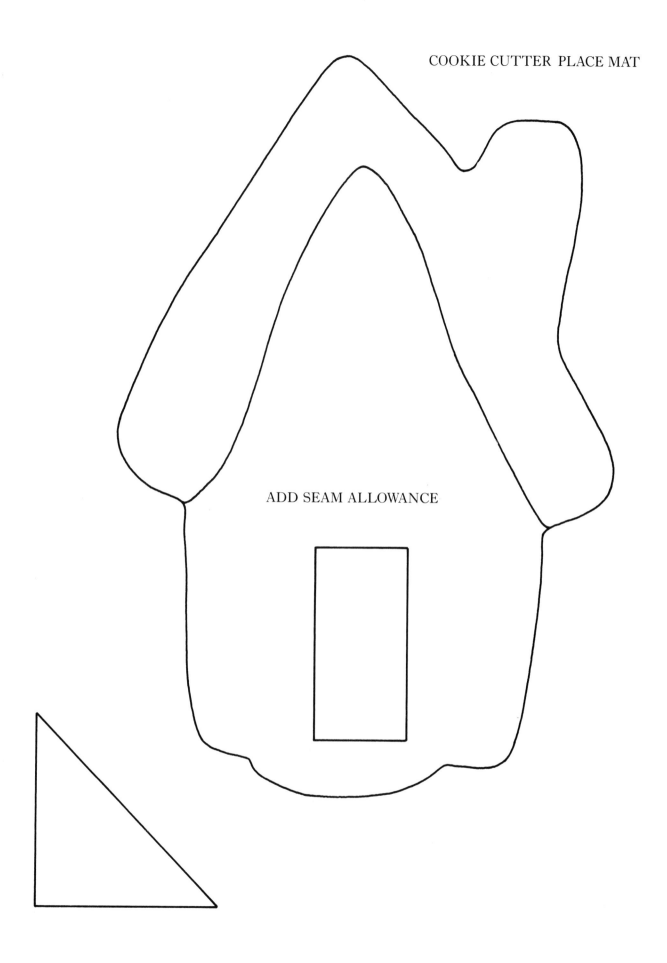

ADD SEAM ALLOWANCE

Tall Pine Tree Place Mat

I used only two colors for this mat, but it is a flexible design. Two or more prints of the same shade could be used for the pine tree, using the same color throughout for the background. The side strips could also be done in a different color, serving as a frame for the center design. You could also choose to use different fabrics for each place mat.

A	8 Dark (4 reverse)	D	10 Dark
	8 Light (4 reverse)		26 Light
B	2 Dark	E	8 Light
C	1 Dark		

Lining: 13″ × 19″

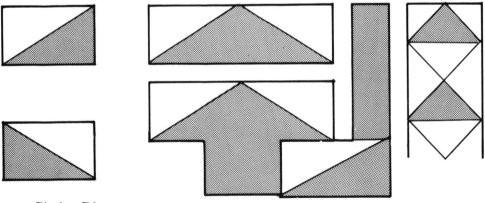

Piecing Diagram

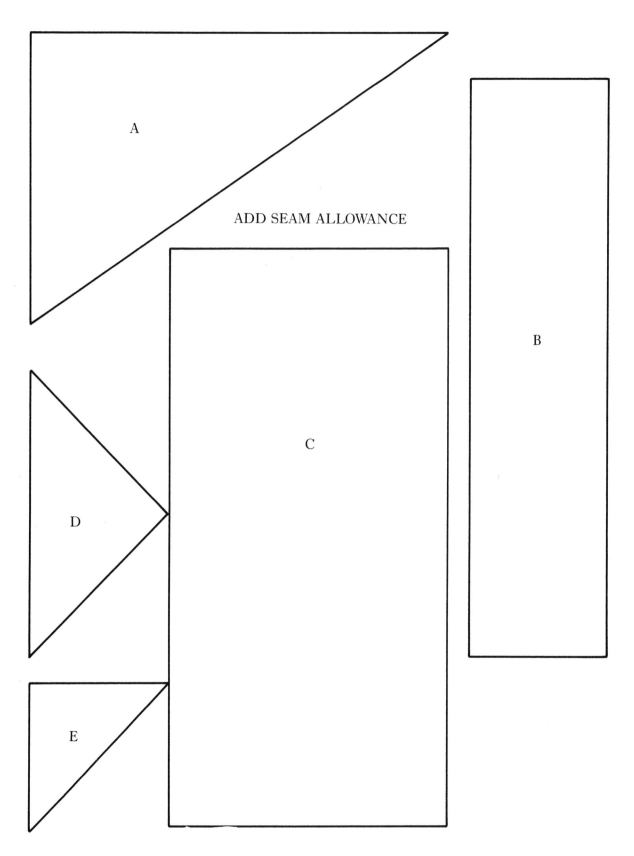

ADD SEAM ALLOWANCE

SPECIAL CHRISTMAS PROJECTS

Tabletop Tree

Here's a quick and easy tree to serve as the centerpiece for your holiday buffet or as a holder to display Christmas cards. I used two different designs for the sides, but you could use just one, or make each side different.

Materials

3 pieces cardboard 18″ × 22″
Assorted scraps
Batting

FOUNDATION

Cut three large triangles measuring 18″ at the base and 22″ high. Use masking tape to tape the three sides together to form a pyramid shape for the tree.

Cut templates for A, B and C.

SIDE 1

Cut fabric strips 3¼″ wide. Seam together two harmonizing or contrasting fabrics. Press seam. To complete the tree as shown, you need three different combinations of fabric. Lay the diamond template B on the assembled fabric strip, lining up the exact center of the template with the seam line. Trace around template and cut out allowing ¼″ to ½″ seam allowance.

Sew four diamonds in a strip, squaring bottom with C triangle (made from half of B). Make second strip using five diamonds and a C triangle.

Repeat above step with the other two sets of fabric. Row two requires a six-diamond strip and a seven-diamond strip, squared off at the bottom with a C triangle.

Row 3 requires an eight-diamond strip and a nine-diamond strip.

ASSEMBLY

Cut out large triangle using template A, adding seam allowance. Sew four-diamond strip to the right-hand side of triangle, then add the five-diamond strip to the left-hand side. Repeat this procedure for the other two fabric combinations. Quilt the completed triangle.

For the second design, I used the *Log Cabin* technique. Cut three strips each of red and green fabric 2″ wide. Cut one strip red and one strip green 3″ wide.

Starting with fabric triangle A, sew a green strip to right-hand side of triangle. Lay the fabric so that it extends beyond the top edge of triangle by about 2″. Cut the top at an angle following the slant of the triangle. Cut bottom edge straight across.

Sew red strip to left-hand side, following the same procedure as above. Repeat, alternating red and green strips. Trim last strips to form a point at top of triangle. Quilt.

Sew the three panels together. Slip it over the cardboard foundation. Turn under bottom edges and staple. If the staples are too noticeable, cover them with a decorative braid or ribbon.

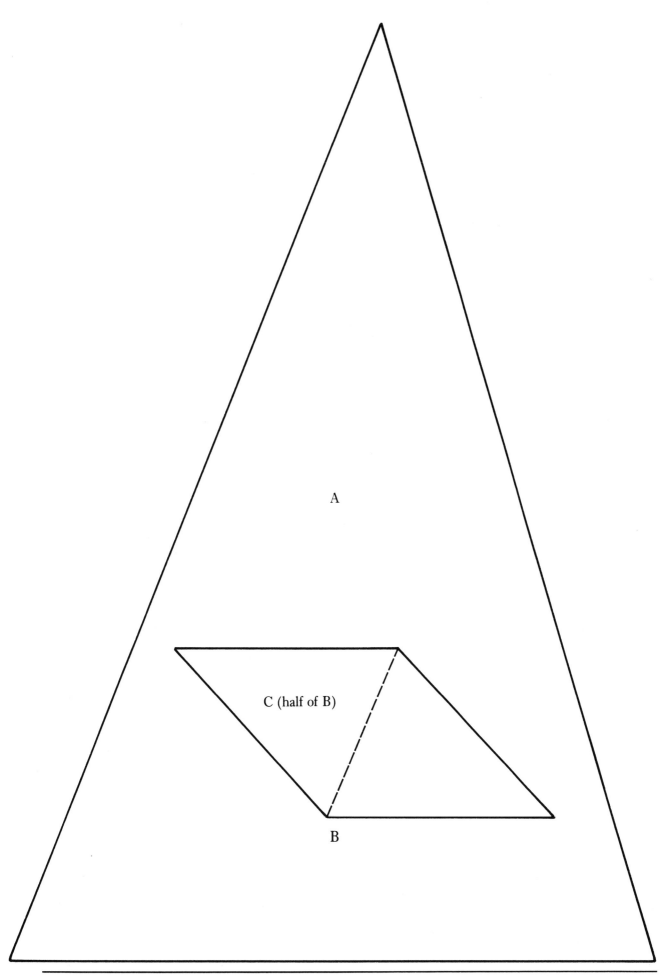

Sleepy Santa Claus Ornament

I used a purchased ornament for the head, but you can make one almost identical with very little effort.

Materials:

2″ Styrofoam ball
face mask
polyester batting
8 ″ piece of gold wire

½ yard red striped fabric
2 chenille stems
Strip of pink fabric

Face

Pin face mask to Styrofoam ball. For glasses, find center of wire. Measure ½″ from center and wrap wire around a pencil to form the lenses. Bend wire back for the stems. Curve center to fit over nose, then push stems into Styrofoam ball.

Glue and pin polyester batting to head, giving Santa a generous head of hair. Repeat for beard.

Fold chenille stem in half and insert folded end into Styrofoam ball. Find center of second chenille stem and wrap it around the first one to form the arms. Wrap arms with pink fabric. Glue to hold.

Body

Cut out patterns for hat, body and sleeves. Place body pattern on fold of fabric and cut out. Repeat for second body piece. Cut two sleeves, placing the fabric so that the stripe runs along the short side and on the hat.

Sew up seams in body, then sew legs. Run a gathering stitch around legs and pull up tight. Gather neck of body and pull tightly around chenille stem.

Gather one end of sleeve. Pull sleeve over arm and tie the thread tightly around wrist. Stitch to body at shoulder.

Sew seam in hat, turn right side out. Finish edge by turning under. You can trim it with a small strip of batting. Make a ball of batting for the tip of the hat. Pin and glue to head.

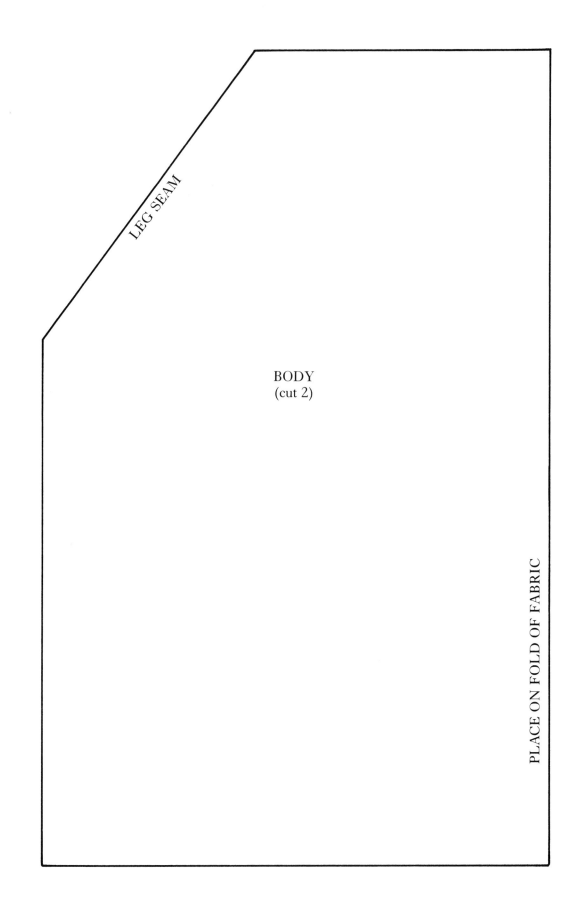

LEG SEAM

BODY
(cut 2)

PLACE ON FOLD OF FABRIC

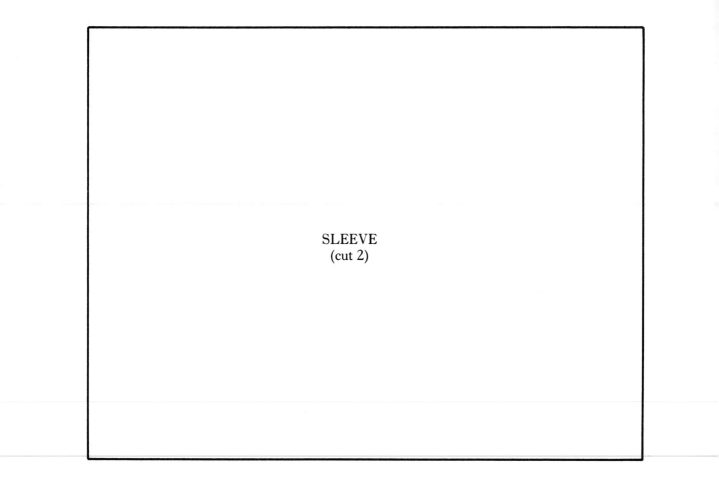

SLEEVE
(cut 2)

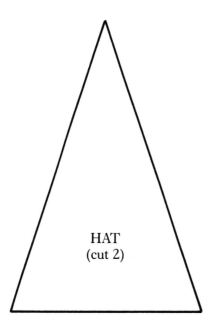

HAT
(cut 2)

Angel Ornament

FULL-SIZE PATTERN

ADD SEAM ALLOWANCE

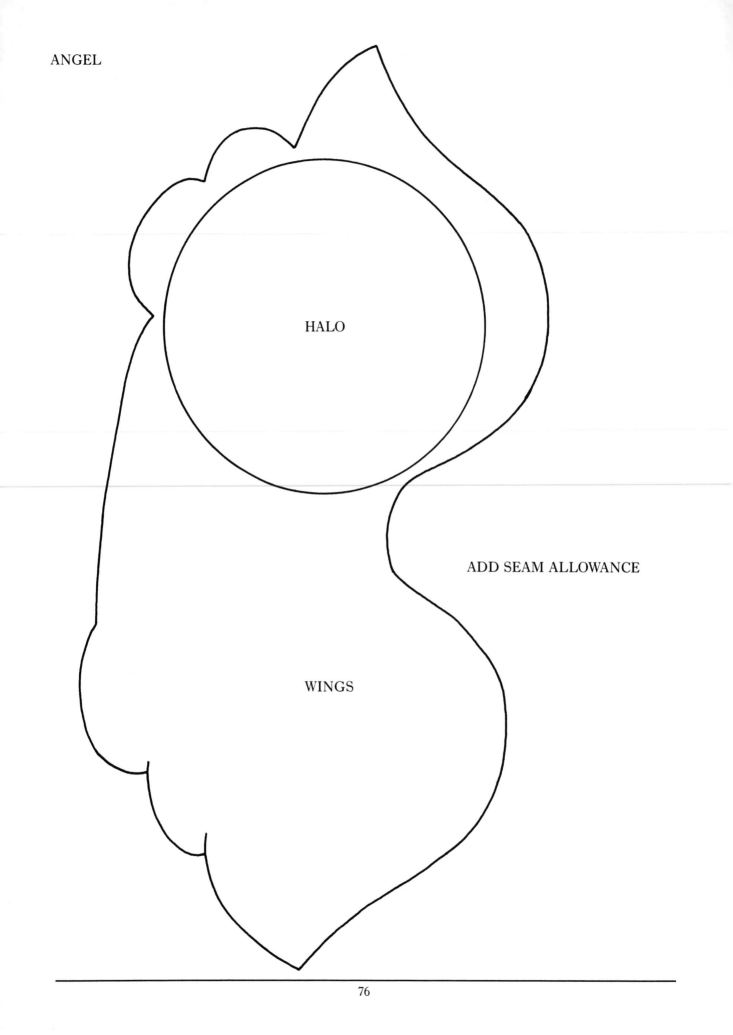

HALO

ADD SEAM ALLOWANCE

WINGS

1. Trace patterns and cut out. From fabric, cut two body pieces, two wings, two halos, one face, and one hand. The hair can be cut from fabric or sewn, using a zigzag satin stitch. From batting, cut out body, wings and halo.

2. Stack batting and fabric for the body, with right sides together. The batting will be on the underside of the stack. Stitch around the body, leaving an opening for turning. Turn to right side and smooth out.

3. Stitch on lines for arms and folds of skirt. Add hands between sleeves.

4. Prepare halo same as you did for the body. Turn right side out and stitch in lines. Sew halo to top of body.

5. Turn under seam allowance on face and sew to halo, just slightly overlapping top of body. Add hair, using either fabric or stitching. Add facial features.

6. Prepare wings as above. When complete, sew it to the body, positioning the upper curve just under the face of the angel on the back. Add cord hanger to top of halo.

Fan Ornament

This is another pattern that lends itself to endless variations.

Cut out ten fan sections and two fan bottoms. Sew five fan sections together for each side. Sew on the fan bottom to each side. Join the two sections, right sides together, leaving an opening for turning. Turn and stuff lightly. Quilt along the seam lines.

Lace, ribbons and flowers can be used for trimming the completed fans.

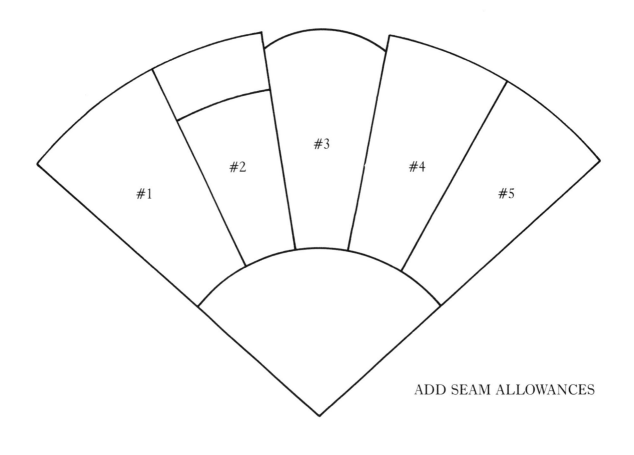

#1 #2 #3 #4 #5

ADD SEAM ALLOWANCES

Six-Point Star Ornament

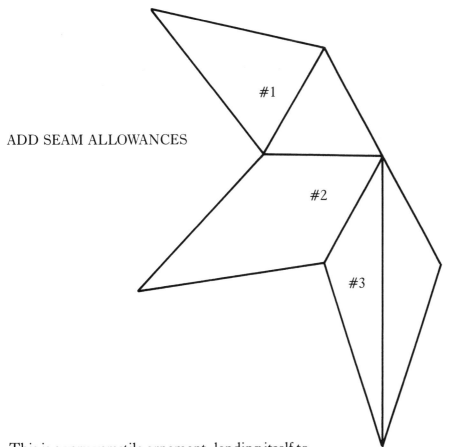

ADD SEAM ALLOWANCES

This is a very versatile ornament, lending itself to many interpretations. On the pattern I have indicated two ways to utilize the fabric.

Side 1: Cut three each of two colors from pattern #2. Sew the star together in the center, making sure you do not sew beyond the seam line.

Side 2: This side uses two fabrics for each point. You can use two fabrics, alternating inner and outer points, or select four fabrics of different colors.

Cut strips of chosen fabrics approximately 4″ wide. Sew two together. Lay pattern pieces #1 and #3 so that the line on the pattern is on the seam line. Cut out. Assemble inner points.

With right sides together, sew the two stars together, leaving an opening for turning. Turn right side out, clipping seams if necessary. Stuff. Sew up seam opening. Attach hanger.

Yo-Yo Tree Ornament

For each tree, cut circles measuring 2″, 4″, 6″, 8″, 9″ and 10″ in diameter.

Take a running stitch around the outside edge of each circle and pull up tightly into a yo-yo.

Beginning with the largest yo-yo, sew them together to form a tree shape. Attach hanger.

Mitten Ornaments

These mittens make a quick and easy last minute project for the tree. They could also be used as a garland or attached to a wreath.

Materials

2 pieces scrap fabric, 6″ × 6″
quilt batting scraps

Make the mitten pattern by tracing onto cardboard. Cut out two shapes for each mitten. There are two ways you can sew them together.

Line the shapes up, right sides out and zigzag stitch around the edges, leaving the top open. Stuff lightly. Or, you can sew them with right sides together, then turn and stuff. The second method makes a slightly smaller mitten. Lay small strips of batting over the open end and sew in place.

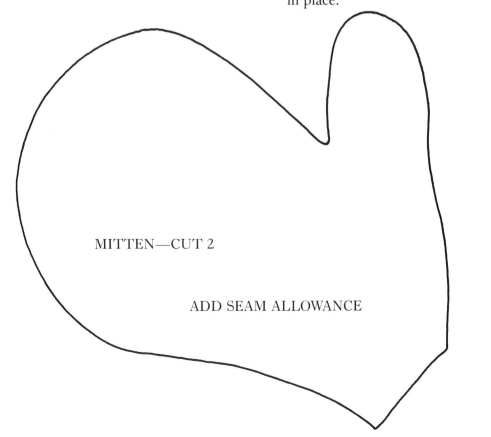

MITTEN—CUT 2

ADD SEAM ALLOWANCE

Gay 90's Stocking

This stocking for your family will add a touch of whimsy to the usual display. After the holidays, the stocking could move to the bedroom to be used as a lingerie bag for dirty stockings.

I have also included a smaller version of the pattern for use as an ornament for the tree, or as a sachet bag.

Stocking

Cut four shoe patterns, being sure to reverse two. Cut two each, A and B appliqués. Add seam allowances.

Lay the A appliqué on the front of the shoe, matching raw edges, and pin to the outside edge. Turn under seam allowance on scalloped edge, clipping curves where necessary. Sew in place with a decorative stitch. Lay heel appliqué, B, in place, raw edges even. Turn under seam allowance on inner curved portion and stitch in place. Repeat for reverse side.

Cut a layer of batting using shoe pattern, then stack the batting, the decorated shoe and the lining, right sides together. Match raw edges of lining and outer shoe and pin the three layers.

Stitch the three layers together, starting at the top edge. Leave the top open for turning. Repeat for second side.

Turn the stocking inside out, clipping seams and curves as needed. Turn under the seam al- lowance on the top edge, and using a decorative stitch, sew around the shoe and across the top. Sew the two completed shoes together leaving the top open.

A

B

Cut two of each pattern piece, being sure to reverse one. Attach appliqués same as for stocking. Sew the two parts of the shoe together, right sides facing, leaving the top edge open for turning. Clip curves and turn right side out. Stuff with batting or potpourri. Close top edge.

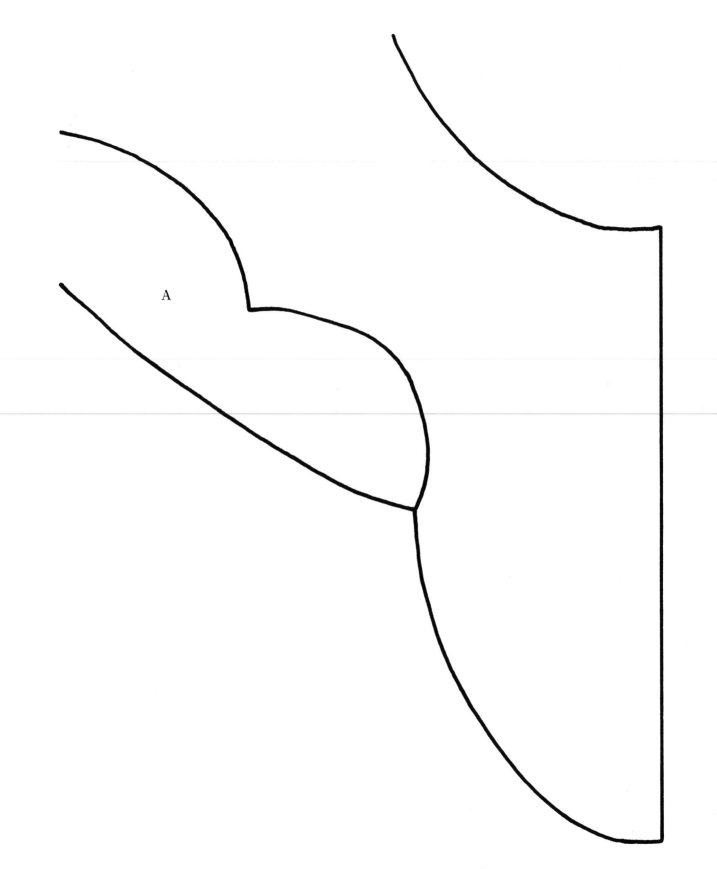

A

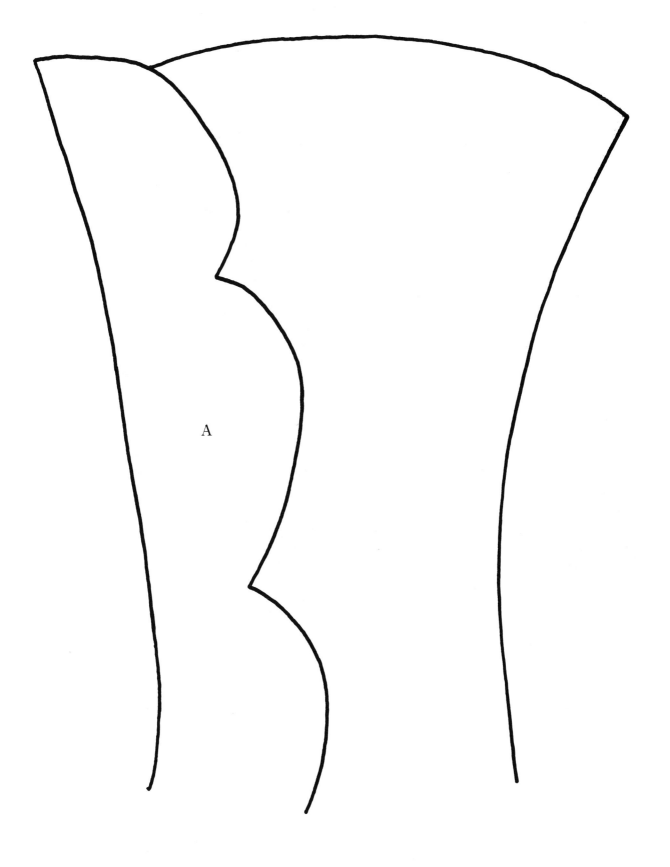

A

Dresden Plate Tree Skirt

Materials

Newspaper sheets taped together to make a
  52″ square
32 6″ × 27″ strips of assorted fabric
Backing fabric 54″ wide—a sheet works fine
Batting
8 yards bias binding
Trims as desired

Making the Pattern

Fold the newspaper sheet into quarters. Cut a
piece of string 27″ long. Tie one end to a pin, the
other end to a pencil, making sure the string is
now 26″ long.

Anchor the pin at the point of the newspaper.
Straighten out the string and draw from side to
side of the newspaper. Cut along the drawn line
(1). Measure down 4″ from the tip and draw
another line from side to side. Cut along this line
(2). This is the pattern for the background material. Do not open the pattern out yet.

To form the "plates" pattern, fold the newspaper so the two sides meet and crease. Repeat
the folding and creasing until the piece measures
about 5″ across at the bottom. Cut out one of
these pieces to serve as the pattern for the plates.

Assembly

Cut out the background fabric and fold and
crease as you did to obtain the pattern. Be sure
the creases are very sharp as this serves as your
seam line as well as your guide in placing the
plates. Cut along one of the lines to open the
circle. This is the back edge.

Cut out the plates, adding seam allowances,
and an equal number of batting pieces cut to
finished size.

Lay the "plate" on the ironing board, right side
down, with the pattern on top. Press the seam
allowance up over the pattern along the bottom
and right side. This will be the left side when
turned over.

Line up the prepared plate with the edge of the
background fabric, being sure the raw edge over-
laps the creased seam line. Select a decorative
stitch, and sew the plate into place along the
outside edge.

Fold back the sewn plate, and place the batting
under it. Smooth the plate back in place. A few
pins are helpful to hold it down. Lay the next
plate, folded edge over the previous raw edge, and
sew in place. Repeat with each plate and batting.

When all the plates have been sewn in position,
bind with bias tape. I sewed gold rickrack over
the tape for a little flash. You could do this or add
some other decorative features as desired.

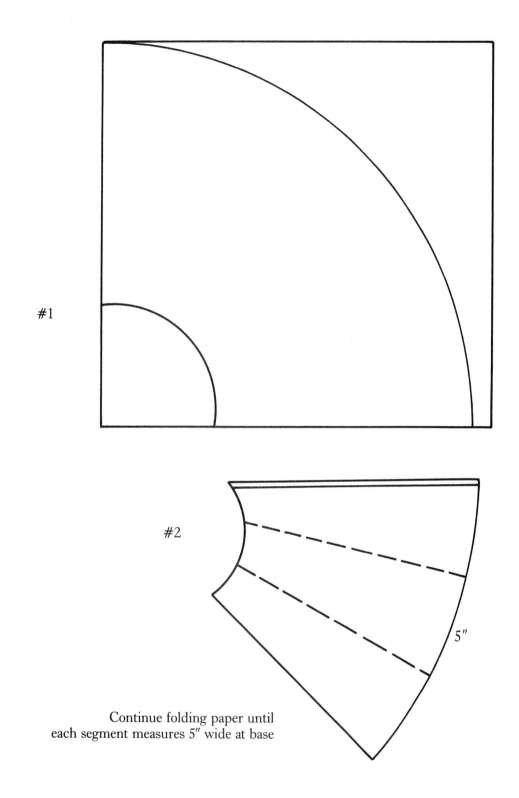

#1

#2

5″

Continue folding paper until
each segment measures 5″ wide at base

Prairie Point Wreath

Materials

Styrofoam or straw wreath form
Assorted fabrics cut in 5″ squares

Fold squares in half diagonally, fold again bringing the points together forming a triangle.

Make a small pleat in center of triangle, then fold ends in to middle. Insert a pin through all layers and pin into the wreath form. I began in the center of the form with two layers, then added the green rows last.

Yo-Yo Wreath

The Yo-Yo Wreath will use up a lot of scrap fabrics, or you might choose to make it up in only two or three colors, such as blue and white or red and green.

Materials

Wreath form, plastic or straw
Assorted fabrics, 6″ square
Fabric bow
Trims—crystal flower beads, gold sequins, pearl-head pins

Cut out a variety of fabrics, using the pattern given. How many you need will depend on the size of your wreath form.

Turn under the raw edges of the circle as you sew, and take a running stitch around the outside edge. Pull the thread up tightly and tie.

Pin the completed yo-yos to the wreath, overlapping so that the wreath does not show. Place the first row on the flat side of the wreath, then work towards the inner and outer curves.

When the wreath is covered, apply the trims. I used a pearl-head pin, with a crystal flower bead and a gold sequin on the bottom, which reflects the light from different angles. You could also try filling the centers with pom-pom balls, and sprinkling the whole thing with diamond dust. Add a fabric bow to complete the wreath.

Bow Tie Wreath

For a last minute decoration, you can't beat this wreath. You can whip it up in just an hour.

Materials

¼ yard green Christmas print
8″ × 36″ red Christmas print

from green, cut 12 A and 6 B
from red, cut 4 A and 2 B

Sew A's to each side of B's to make four Bow Ties. Repeat with remaining pieces for the back of the wreath.

Sew the completed Bow Ties together to form the wreath.

RIBBON

Cut strip of fabric 4″ by 36″. Fold 36″ length in half and fold in half again. Cut one end on the diagonal. Cut through the folded edge. Sew two pieces together along the sides and bottom. Turn.

Repeat for second ribbon. Gather the raw edges slightly to fit on the square of the red bow. Pin to the right side of the fabric, with the ribbons going into the wreath.

Pin the backing to the front of the bow along the outer edge. Sew around, catching in the ribbons. Clip corners and turn right side out.

Press under raw edges of inner ring. Stuff wreath and whipstitch the inside closed.

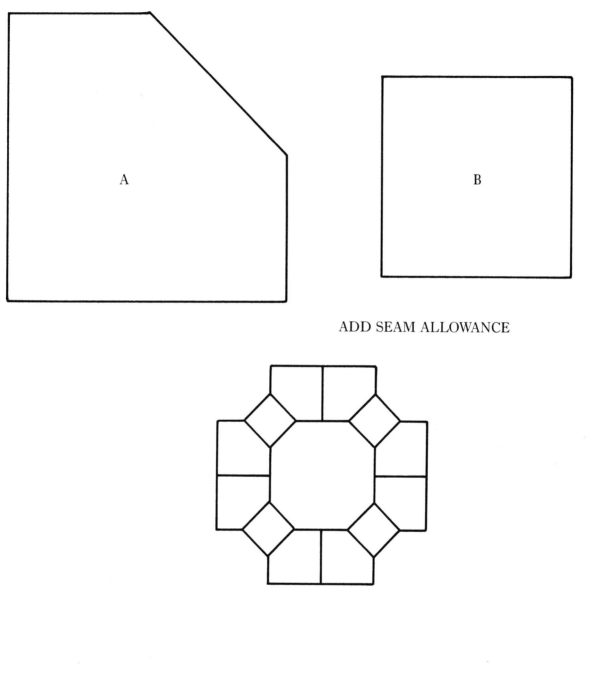

A

B

ADD SEAM ALLOWANCE

Chalet

The Chalet, shown in the color section, was adapted from a design for a gingerbread house. An entire village can be made by adapting these patterns to fabric, which would be attractive under a tree. It was also suggested to me that this particular pattern would make a nice toaster cover for the holidays (or for that matter, a great gift wrap). In fact, why not make covers for all your appliances, using this idea.

Patterns

House front and back: see diagram

House sides: 5″ × 9″
Roof: 11″ × 17″
Door: 1½″ × 2½″ (round off one corner)
Lower Shutters: 1″ × 2″
    Window   1″ × 1″
Middle Shutters: 1½″ × 3″
    Window   1½″ × 2¾″
Upper Shutters: 1″ × 1¾″
    Window   1″ × 1″

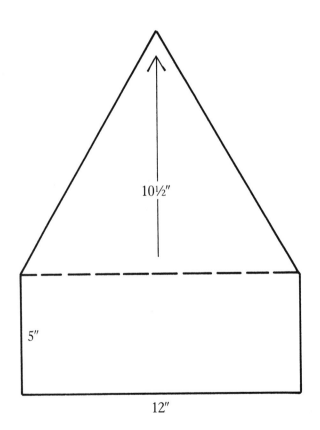

10½″

5″

12″

Add seam allowances to each pattern and cut the following from fabric:

House front and back—4
House sides—4
Roof—4

Lower Shutters—4	Lower windows—2
Middle Shutters—2	Middle window—1
Upper Shutters—2	Upper window—1

From cardboard, cut front, back and two sides. Appliqué door, windows and shutters to front of house. For village display: Lay a piece of batting under house front and quilt a design on the fabric. Repeat for back and sides. When quilting is finished, take lining fabric and sew to each piece, right sides facing. Leave the bottom of each piece open. Insert cardboard between the layers of fabric and close the bottom seam. Join the sides to front and back. Sew on roof.

For an appliance cover, sew front to lining, turn; insert batting and quilt. Repeat for each piece, then join the pieces to form the house. Sew on roof.

Checkerboard and Backgammon Board

Backgammon Board

From A, cut 12 light
12 medium
20 dark

Cut A in half lengthwise, add seam allowance, and cut eight dark. Sew the A's together as illustrated.

Cut a 3″-wide strip of dark and sew two completed squares together as shown.

Cut a 2″-wide strip of light. Sew to the long side of each piece.

Cut flannel to the size of the three completed pieces. Lay each section on top of the flannel and quilt along the seams. Turn under ½″ on the light strips, fold the strip in half and turn to the underside. Stitch in place.

On the backgammon sections, cut a 4″-wide strip for the border. Pin the two sections together, overlapping the light center strips. Sew the border to the edges.

Checkerboard

½ yard dark
½ yard light
½ yard medium

Select two strongly contrasting fabrics and cut three 3″-wide strips from each. Using a half-inch seam allowance, sew two dark and two light strips together, alternating colors.

Press the "fabric," and cut apart every 3″. This makes fourteen strips. Cut the two remaining strips in half and sew them together as before. Press and cut two 3″ wide strips.

Sew together four strips, alternating colors in each row. Make four such squares. Sew the four completed squares together to form the checkerboard.

From the light fabric, cut two strips 3½″ wide and sew around the outer edge of the checkerboard. Set aside.

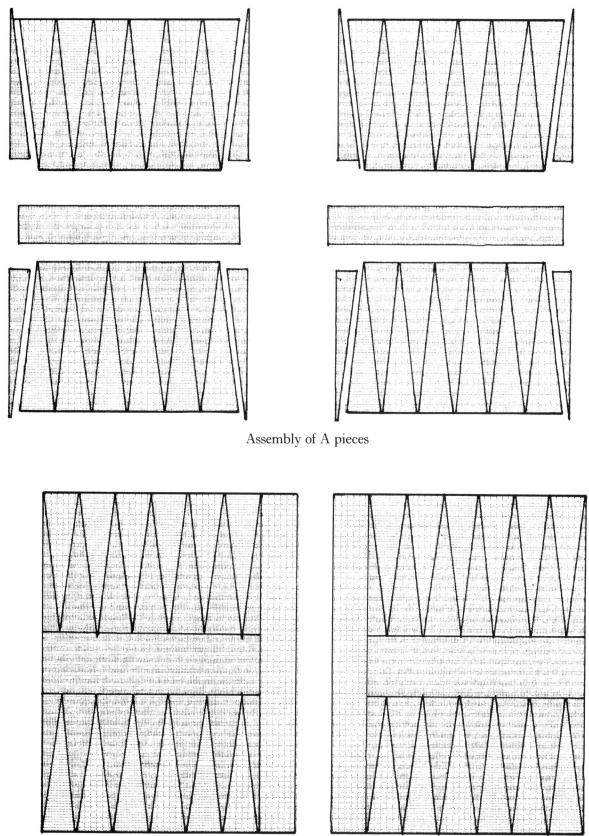

Assembly of A pieces

with inside border attached

Checkers

Cut twelve dark and twelve light 3″ circles. Cut twenty-four 2½″ circles of batting. Take a running stitch around the outer edge of the circles, place batting in center of circle and pull thread up tight. Tie. Store checkers inside the board.

Pin the backgammon and checkerboard sections together, right sides facing. Sew around the outer edge. Turn right side out through the opening in the backgammon section.

Quilt the border.

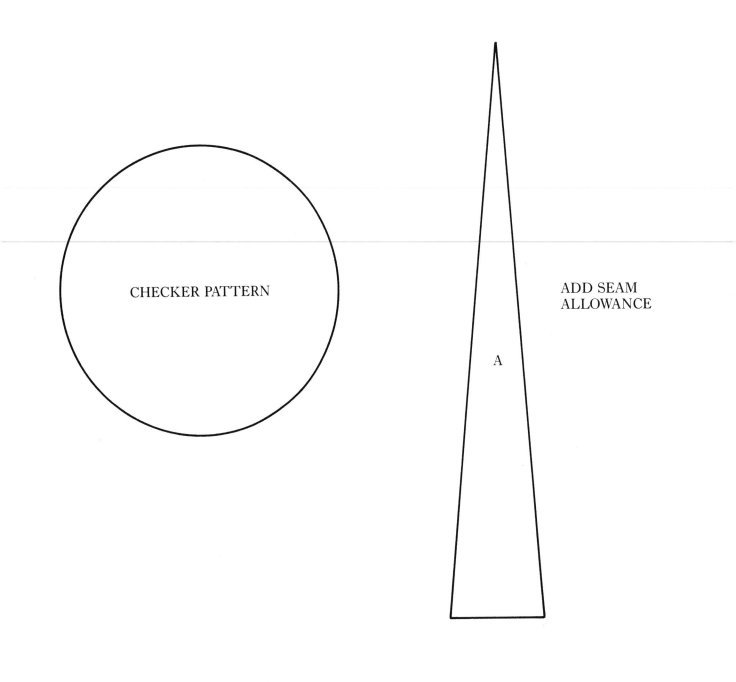

CHECKER PATTERN

ADD SEAM
ALLOWANCE

A

April's Valentine

My eight-year-old daughter April, came up with this design. It is so simple that she was able to put it together by herself with just a little help from me. It took about six hours from start to finish to complete the piece shown, so it is a fast pattern to make. When I'm ready to finish the quilt, I'll add some borders to bring it up to crib size.

I don't usually have many pastel colors around, so I did purchase the background fabric especially for this design. An alternative though, would be to use two or more pastel colors for the background blocks, then use one color for the hearts throughout.

1. Cut out four triangles for each square. Add seam allowances to the pattern given. The piece shown has 16 squares.
2. Cut out several strips of white fabric that will measure ¾″ wide, plus seam allowance.

Log Cabin Border

Select six harmonizing fabrics, three light, three medium to dark. Cut two strips 4″ wide from each fabric. Cut a third strip from the two colors that will form the outside border.

Begin at the top with the lightest color strip and sew it across. Bring the same color down the right side. At the bottom, switch to the lightest darker colors, and sew it around the remaining two sides. Repeat with the other colors to form the *Log Cabin* border. (The third strip is necessary to make the outside strips long enough to go around.)

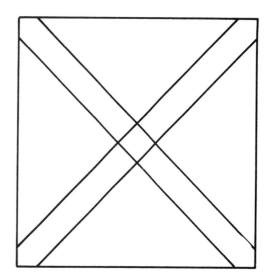

PIECING DIAGRAM

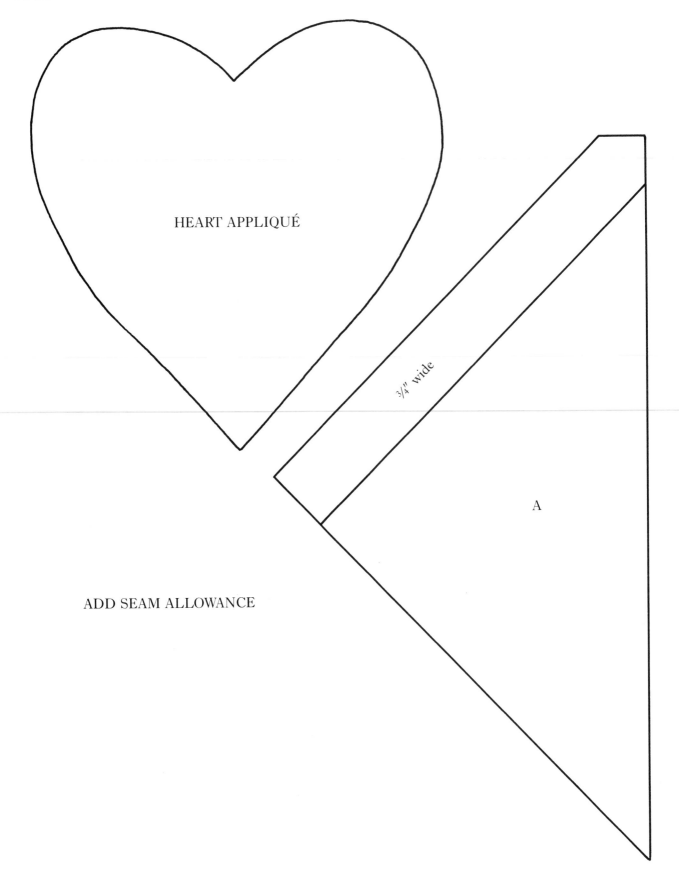

HEART APPLIQUÉ

¾" wide

A

ADD SEAM ALLOWANCE

Potholders

All of the potholders shown are assembled in the same way. The inside lining is used to help insulate the potholder so you don't burn yourself.

Make a paper pattern for each element of the design, adding seam allowances to pattern. From fabric, cut two of each. Using flannel or some other heavier fabric, cut two of the major design element without the seam allowance.

Lay the lining fabric on the wrong side of each major shape and tack it in the center. Align the shapes.

Sew any appliqué pieces onto the larger shape.

Cut one or two, if you prefer, of the large shape from batting, omitting seam allowance. Sew the front and back of the shapes together, right sides together, leaving an opening for turning. Turn right side out.

Quilt any designs desired onto the shape. Turn in the raw edges of the opening and sew closed.

Daisy

Select ¼ yard pieces of two fabrics. Fold the fabrics in half, right sides facing. Draw around the petal shape eight times on each fabric. Sew the two layers together on the drawn line. Cut out, clip curves and turn. Stuff lightly with batting. Overlap the base of the petals and pin in place as you go to form a circle. Sew along the edge of the overlapped edges, stopping where the petals meet at the outside edge. Turn the mat over and sew the opposite side in the same way. Sew a circle in the center of each side.

Cup

Using a half-inch seam allowance, cut a 5½″ wide light center strip, 2½″ wide print bottom strip and a 2″ wide top strip. Sew the strips together, press and cut out the cup pattern from the assembled fabric. The hole in the handle is quilted in.

Flower

For a perfect circle in the center, cut out the center from fabric, adding seam allowance. Take a running stitch along the outside edge of the circle. Make a cardboard pattern of the circle and lay it in the center of the fabric. Pull up the basting thread tightly around the cardboard. Press. Remove cardboard and appliqué in place.

Exercise Mat

The first mat I made was designed as a cover for a rattan rocking chair. It had a pillow to sit on, but the back was very uncomfortable to lean against. It just happened that when I began exercising, the chair mat was handy to throw on the floor. I like things that serve a dual purpose.

That mat has long since worn out, so I made one specifically for exercising. My little boy also likes to take naps on it. This mat makes a great gift for someone who has just taken up exercising.

For this mat, I used the blocks I had made for a quilt I knew I would never finish. (I don't know what possessed me to buy some of this fabric, but I did know that I didn't want to look at it on a bed.) If you have an unfinished quilt, try using it for this item, or select an assortment of blocks, or design a special top. The top should measure about 36″ × 60″.

I like a lot of padding if I'm on the floor, so I added 3″-wide strips to the top to allow for 2″ of padding. Cut a backing piece the same size as the top. Do not include the strips in this measurement. Sew the backing to the strips on three sides. Turn right side out. You have a 2″-gap now for the padding.

Stuff with quilt batting, being sure to keep the sides squared. You're forming a boxlike shape as in the pillow. Close the last seam.

If you prefer less padding, make the mat the same way you would a quilt, with maybe a little extra padding. Tie the layers together to maintain the loft.

Kids love to sleep on the floor and this mat is ideal for the purpose. You could also try a sleeping bag.

Sleeping Bag

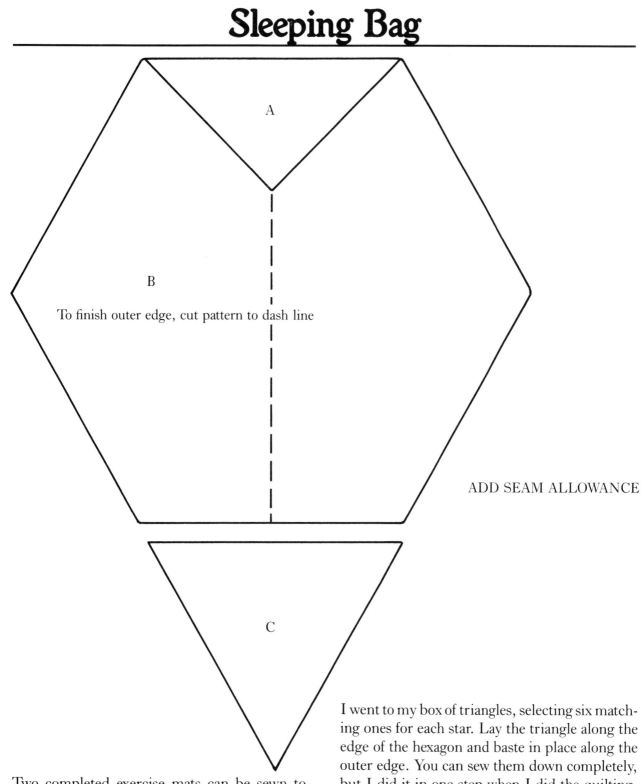

A

B

To finish outer edge, cut pattern to dash line

ADD SEAM ALLOWANCE

C

Two completed exercise mats can be sewn together to form a sleeping bag for a child. Both mats measure approximately 36″ × 48″ and can be seen in the Color Section.

Side one, which I call *Under the Stars*, evolved from the *Brilliant Star* pattern and is assembled the same way. To form the stars on each hexagon,

I went to my box of triangles, selecting six matching ones for each star. Lay the triangle along the edge of the hexagon and baste in place along the outer edge. You can sew them down completely, but I did it in one step when I did the quilting.

You will need 72 yellow hexagons and 432 assorted triangles, in six different colors. Assemble in rows with the red triangles.

To square the edges, sew the partial hexagons along the outside, filling in between the triangles.

Side two, *Moon Over the City*, uses 3″ squares (A) for the bottom half, and a *Log Cabin* type mountain for an enlarged *Moon Over the Mountain* top half.

I strip-pieced the squares, then cut them apart and assembled them in staggered rows. It takes one 3½″ strip of 12 different fabrics, cut across the width of the fabric.

For the top half, you will need ½ yard of fabric for the background (see piecing diagram). Mark the exact center along the bottom edge. Cut out a 3″ triangle (B) (*Be sure to add seam allowance*). Lay a 3½″ wide strip of fabric along the triangle, right sides facing, matching seam lines, and lining the strip up with the top edge of the triangle. Stitch in place. Turn the strip right side up and press.

Lay a second strip on the opposite side of the triangle, placing it so that it matches the outer edge of the previously sewn strip. Continue in this manner until you have added four strips to each side. Don't worry about the length of the strips at this point, they will be cut off later.

For the moon, cut out a 20″ diameter circle of yellow fabric.

Position the mountain on the background fabric, matching the center you marked and the center of the triangle. Pin in place along the bottom edge. Smooth out the mountain and pin here and there to hold. Cut off any excess strips even with the bottom edge. Place the moon behind the mountain and pin to hold. Turn under all seam allowances and pin. Stitch in place. Join the top and bottom halves together. Quilt. Finish both quilts as if they are to be separate quilts.

Lay one quilt on top of the other, linings together. Sew down one side, across the bottom and one-third to one-half way up the other side. If you want the bag to close on the open side, attach Velcro strips to each surface of the lining.

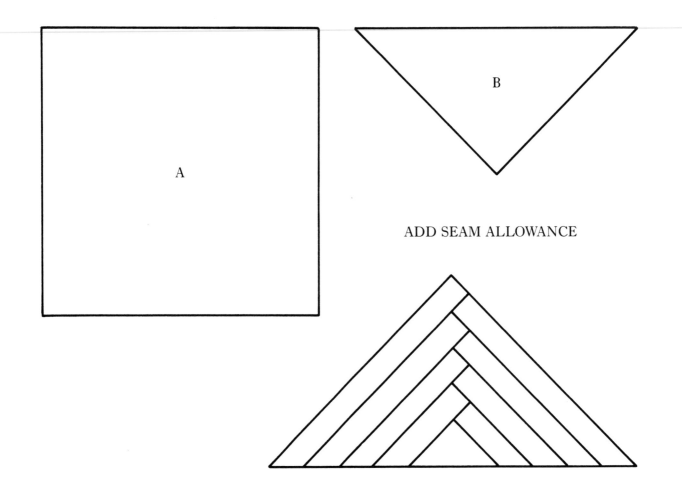

ADD SEAM ALLOWANCE

Padded Hanger

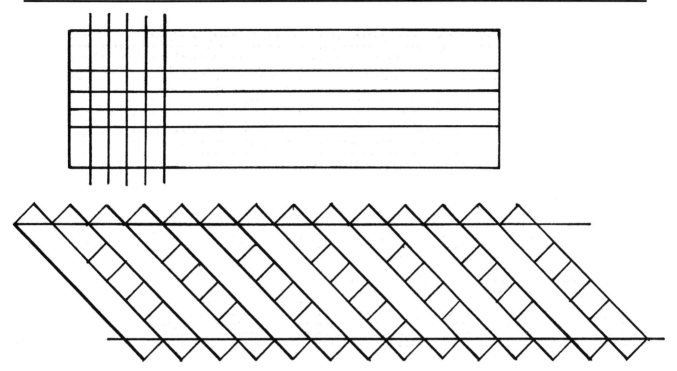

A padded hanger is your knitwear's best friend. It's quick and easy to make, and is also great as a small gift or bazaar item. I've used Seminole patchwork for this one, but design possibilities are endless. Try some floral appliqués for a truly dainty set of hangers.

Materials

1 plastic hanger
quilt batting (leftovers are fine)
2 strips print #1—2½″ × 36″
1 strip print #1—1½″ × 36″
2 strips print #2—1½″ × 36″
4 strips coordinating fabric 2″ × 36″
2 strips #2 coordinating fabric 3″ × 36″

Sew the first five strips of fabric together as shown above.

Cut the sewn strips apart every 2″. Cut the coordinating fabric into pieces 7″ long. Sew the strips together as illustrated. Make 2. Press thoroughly. Sew the #2 coordinating fabric to top and bottom of the completed strips.

Cut strips of batting approximately 1″ wide and wrap the plastic frame of the hanger. Do not wrap the hook. Cut a piece of batting large enough to cover the wrapped portion of the hanger solidly and smooth the batting into place. You may want to add a second layer of batting for additional padding. Baste the padding in place.

I haven't provided a pattern for the hanger because they do vary in size. You will also have a variance, depending on how much padding is applied. Lay the padded hanger on a large sheet of paper and resting your pencil lightly along the outer edge, trace around it from bottom of hook to opposite bottom of hook. Don't press in on the batting. If the pattern looks a little rough, fold it in half, centering the hook section. Cut it out, smoothing out any wavy or rough edges as you cut.

Center the pattern on the strips and cut out two, adding seam allowance as you cut. Fold down the seam allowance where the hook comes out, and sew the two pieces together, right sides facing, from the hook edge to slightly around the rounded bottom edge. Clip curves. Turn right side out. Insert padded hanger and sew bottom opening closed.

Garment Cover

Making your own garment covers for seldom-worn or out-of-season clothing allows you to add a bright touch to your closets as well as having them appear well organized. The covers are simple to make and can be embellished with any type of trim or decoration you have on hand. For this example, I used a quilt top that didn't turn out quite the way I planned. Any patchwork design, including crazy quilting, would work well. You could also choose an appliqué design, or practice your quilting stitches by making a cover in your favorite color and quilting the design on.

The length of the cover can vary depending on what you want to store. Measure the garment and adjust the cover accordingly.

Materials

1 plastic coat hanger
Pieced, appliqué or plain fabric large enough to cut two sides

Lay the hanger on a large sheet on paper and trace around it. Add 1″ around the edges of the hanger down to the curve. Draw a straight line from the curve to the length desired. This is your pattern.

Cut two from fabric. Quilt the fabric. Turn down the top area where the hanger hook comes through. Sew the two sides together, right sides facing. Turn right side out and hem.

This can also be made to accommodate more than one hanger by adding a strip of fabric at the seam. See the illustration below.

Chair Caddy

This caddy was designed to help keep track of the remote control devices for the TV and VCR as well as the *TV Guide*. There is also a pocket for magazines or whatever you want to use it for. You can customize it for whatever uses you may have. The caddy is also adaptable to any type chair since it is designed to fit over the arm and under the seat cushion. It is shown in the color section.

2 strips background fabric 19″ × 49″
First pocket—2 strips 13″ × 19″
TV Guide pocket—2 strips 9″ × 11″
Remote control pockets—2 strips 10″ × 6½″

Pockets

Sew the guide pocket together along top and right side. Turn. Place batting in center and quilt.

Remote pockets. Sew two pieces together along top and left side. Turn and quilt.

Large pocket. Stack the two pieces with batting in between and quilt. The sides will be unfinished. Across the top sew a ¾″ wide binding.

Backing. Stack the two long pieces right sides out with the batting in the middle. Quilt.

Assembly

Position the small pockets on the larger pocket and sew in place. Find the center of the remote pocket and sew a line from top to bottom. This creates two pockets.

Place the assembled pockets at one end of the backing and stitch both sides and across the bottom.

Cut binding strips 5″ wide × 136″ long. Fold the strip in half. Sew the raw edges of the binding to the raw edges of the backing. Turn the folded edge over to the back and stitch in place.

Wall Basket

This makes a nice decoration for holding an arrangement of dried flowers. Directions are also given to make a matching place mat, or it would make a pretty full-size quilt.

For the band across the top, cut two strips of solid fabric 2″ wide by 18″ long; one strip of print 2″ × 18″. Sew the three strips together, the print in the middle. Cut apart every two inches.

Lay one segment on the table. Align the next segment: solid square next to print square. Continue across until you have eight such segments. Sew them together.

Press the strip. Lay your ruler one half inch above the top of the points, and cut off excess. Repeat for bottom of strip. Set aside.

Cut one A from fabric chosen for basket bottom. Be sure to add seam allowance. Cut three B from same fabric.

Sew the strip previously made to the top of A. Press and lay it on your cutting mat. Align your ruler along the sides of the basket and cut away excess fabric from strip.

Handle

Cut one strip each of three fabrics 6″ × 24″. Fold each strip in half. Press. Fold the raw edge to the middle of the strip, then fold the folded edge over the raw edge. Press. Braid the three strips together, pinning each end to hold.

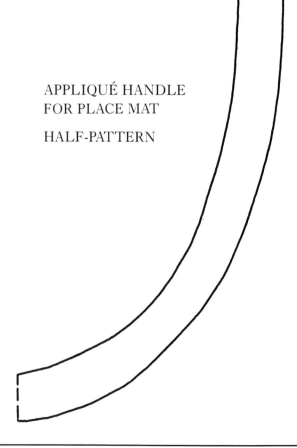

APPLIQUÉ HANDLE
FOR PLACE MAT

HALF-PATTERN

APPLIQUÉ BOW FOR PLACE MAT

ADD SEAM ALLOWANCE

Ribbon

Cut a strip 4″ × 36″. Stitch along long edge. Turn right side out. Make four loops for the bow. Gather in the center and tie tightly. Wrap a scrap of fabric around the center and sew in place. Fold the remains of the strip in half lengthwise and cut. On the wrong side, sew a slanted seam on one end of each strip. Turn right side out and sew to the back of the bow. See bow to basket handle.

For place mats or a quilt, use the patterns given for the bow and handle.

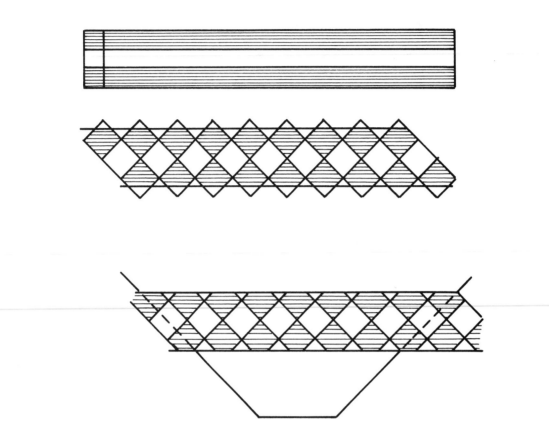

Basket Back

Cut one B from batting. Cut the braided handle 14″ long. Pin the handle to the right side of a fabric B, raw edges even. Place the batting on the wrong side of the remaining B and pin the two layers to B, right sides together. Stitch around the sides and top. Turn. Quilt in a diagonal design.

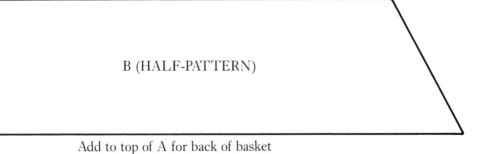

B (HALF-PATTERN)

Add to top of A for back of basket

Basket Front

Stack the pieced B face down on the last B piece. Place batting on top. Stitch around three sides. Turn and quilt.

A

ADD SEAM ALLOWANCE

Checkbook Cover

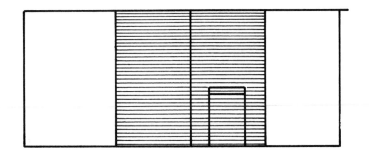

This cover can be made in less than an hour, which makes it a good candidate for bazaar sales. It also sports a small pocket on the front in which to keep identification for check cashing.

I used denim for this cover, but you can also quilt a small remnant and use that.

Materials

Denim from old blue jeans 7″ × 15″ (I used a leg)
1 piece cotton fabric 7″ × 15″
1 piece denim 3¼″ × 3¼″ (cut so that the top edge is on the double-sewn seam of the leg)
For a quilted cover, cut two pieces of pocket fabric 3¾″ × 3¾″.

DENIM COVER

Fold the denim in half and mark. Lay the pocket fabric along the mark, even with the side edge. Zigzag-stitch the pocket in place.

Lay the lining and outer fabric together, right sides facing. Starting at one pocket edge, stitch around the cover, stopping at the other pocket edge. Clip corners. Turn right side out.

Fold each end of cover to within ½″ of center. Pin. Stitch ¼″ from each edge.

QUILTED COVER

44″ of bias binding

Select pattern for outer cover. A strip of Seminole patchwork would look beautiful on the side opposite the pocket. Sandwich the cover top, batting and lining together, and quilt.

Sew the two pocket pieces together, wrong side out, along both sides and the top. Turn right side out. Lay the pocket along the center line, raw edges even with the side. Zigzag-stitch pocket in place. Finish edges with bias binding.

Turn both ends to the center and pin ½″ from the center line. Sew ¼″ along both edges.

Beach Blanket Tote

This little blanket is a whiz to whip up, especially if you have a stash of half-square triangles already cut. It features four pockets to carry those small items you need at the beach. For true luxury, back it with terrycloth. You can see it in the color section.

Join the half-square triangles with white triangles to form a square. Assemble according to the diagram below.

UNIT 1

	Need 4	total
Six 2″ triangle squares		24
Two 3″ × 7″ light strips		8
One 3″ × 5″ dark strip		4
Two 2″ triangle squares to match dark strip		8

Follow diagram for assembly.

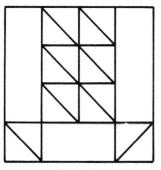

Unit 1

9″ square

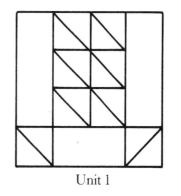

Unit 1

Row 1

UNIT 2

Need 20
Four 2″ triangle squares

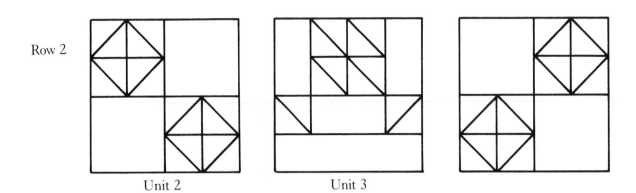

Row 2

Unit 2   Unit 3

UNIT 3

	Need 6	
Four 2″ triangle squares		24
Two 3″ × 5″ light strips		12
One 3″ × 5″ dark strip		6
Two 2″ triangle squares to match		
dark strip		12
One 3″ × 9″ light strip		

Follow diagram to assemble.

Cut three 9″ navy squares
Cut twenty-four 5″ navy squares

Assembly

Row 1: Join two Unit 1s to either side of a 9″ navy square. Make two rows.

Row 2: Join pieced unit 2 to 5″ navy square. Repeat three more times and arrange according to above diagram.

Join these completed units to either side of a Unit 3 (ship-design block). Make two rows.

Sew row 2 to row 1.

Row 3: This row is three squares deep to allow for placement of the pockets.

Join two unit 2s together and sew to top of unit 3.

Cut four 5″ × 9″ rectangles. Turn under ¾″ on 5″ edge and hem.

Sew together two 5″ blue squares and two pieced Unit 2s.

Lay the two blue squares lengthwise and place the unhemmed edge of the pocket even with the bottom edge of the squares. Lay one of the pieced units on top of the pocket, blue square at the top. Sew along the right edge. (For the opposite side, sew along the left edge.) Make four. Sew the second set of blue/pieced blocks to the bottom of the finished unit.

Sew these on either side of the ship block you made earlier.

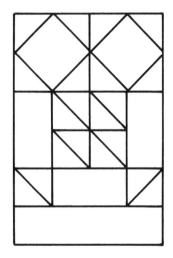

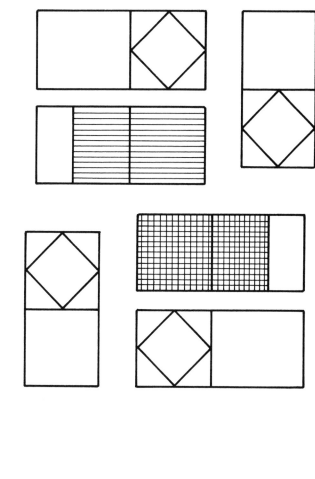

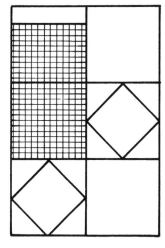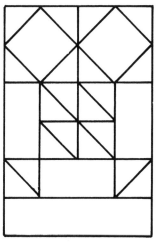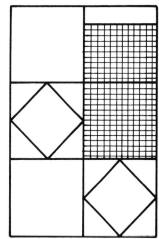

Row 3

Row 4: Sew two Unit 3s to each side of a 9″ square.

Sew on the other three rows to complete the design area.

BORDERS

Cut four strips of red, white and blue fabric 3″ wide. Sew two strips of each color together to get the 64″ length you need. Sew to the edges of the top.

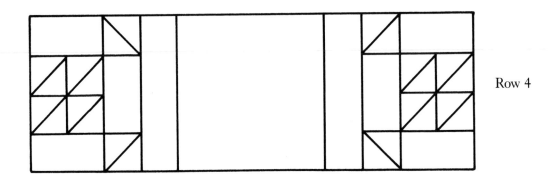

Row 4

TIE

Cut a strip 3″ × 48″. Sew raw edges together along the length of the strip. Turn. Turn in ends and sew across.

Finishing

2 yards terrycloth or backing of choice
2 yards very thin batting
Tie
Fold the top into quarters. Mark one side of top edge at the quarter mark with a pin. Fold the tie in half and pin the folded end at the pin mark.

The fold should be at the seam line with the ties inside the sandwich. Spread out the backing and lay the top face down. Spread the batting over the top. Sew around three sides of the sandwich. Turn right side out.

I used minimal quilting, by quilting only around the solid blue squares. This is just enough to keep the three layers from shifting too much. Quilt down the inside of the red border to facilitate folding the border in when rolling the mat.

To roll the mat, fold the borders to the back. Then fold in half and roll up from the bottom. Wrap the tie around the roll and tie.

Rose Trellis Appliqué Screen

This screen was something of an emergency measure to keep my two-year-old from going behind the computer and turning it off. For the frame I used an old swinging door I had, but you can find ready-made frames at your local hardware store or make them yourself to fit the area you want to cover. Three panels are usually used, but you can use as many as you wish for the particular area you have in mind. It can be seen in the Color Section.

Measure the inside dimensions of your frame. Select a pattern that will fit into the dimensions. Mine measured 13″ × 33″. The *Rose Trellis* design was an 11″ block, but by making the stems a little longer, I could stretch it to fit the area. This is the main advantage of using an appliqué design for this project. Most patterns can be stretched or scrunched to fit the area, but a pieced pattern must be exactly the right size.

Cut the background fabric approximately 2″ larger than the opening. Sew the appliqué pattern in place and quilt as usual.

To attach the quilted panel to the frame, you will need some thin, 1″ wide pieces of wood. A very heavy cardboard would also work. Cut a strip of the wood for each side of the frame, measuring ¼″ smaller than the length and width of your frame. The purpose of the wood strips is to help you pull the fabric evenly taut.

Begin at the top and place the fabric panel inside the frame. Smooth it out and position it evenly. Lay the wood strip on top of the fabric and nail or staple it to the frame. Do the sides next, working back and forth to ensure that the fabric is smooth with no distortions, then finish the bottom edge in the same way.

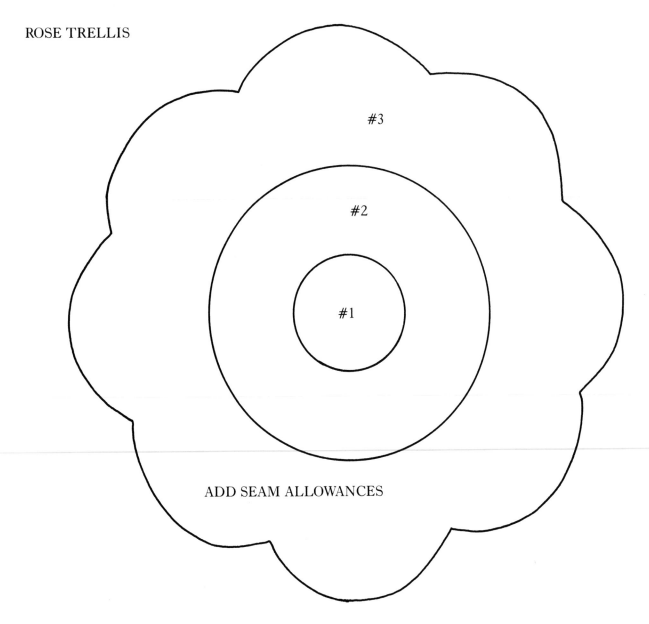

#3

#2

#1

ADD SEAM ALLOWANCES

For stems, cut 2″ wide bias strips. Fold outside
edges to center; fold again. Press.

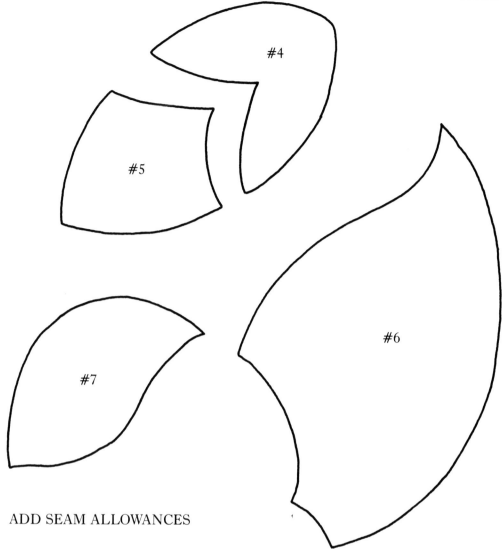

#4

#5

#6

#7

ADD SEAM ALLOWANCES

Fire Screen

A fire screen is a nice decorative touch to cover that gaping hole in the wall during the summer months. And if you have a fireplace that isn't functional, you can go wild making one for each season or even for each month of the year.

For this one, I used an unfinished *Giant Dahlia* quilt top that had been around here for four or five years. The circular shape dictated the method I used to assemble it into a screen, but you can make the screen any shape desired. For a square or rectangular screen, you will need to build a wood frame to the proper dimensions, then mount the quilted design in the frame in the same manner as for the Rose Trellis design or, if you don't want the wood to show, wrap the quilt around the frame and nail to the back. My version can be seen in the Color Section.

I had the center design of the *Giant Dahlia* already pieced, so I folded it in half and quilted it. The outside edge was folded under and stitched to form a casing. Half-inch PVC pipe was pushed through the casing, which maintains the curve of the screen. For the base I used a four-foot length of 4″ × 4″ wood with ½″ holes drilled in each end. The ends of the PVC pipe fit into the holes in the wood to hold it upright.

Cosmetic Case

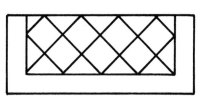 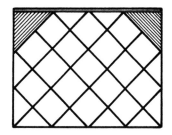

This cosmetic case uses a Seminole type patchwork, but you could use any design you prefer.

Materials

2 3″ × 36″ strips of four fabrics
1 3″ × 36″ contrasting strip
¼ yd. lining fabric

Sew the four fabric strips together. Press and cut apart every 3″. Using five strips, sew them together, dropping down one square for each strip. Lay the finished strip on your cutting board. Position the ruler ½″ above the point of the strip and cut off excess. Repeat for bottom. Even up sides so your resulting rectangle will measure approximately 10″. This is the front of the case. Cut a piece of lining material the same size.

For the back and flap of the case, sew together eight strips of fabric. Cut into 3″ strips and sew together as you did for the front. Press. Cut piece to measure 9″ × 10″. Cut flap edge as shown in illustration. The front edge will measure 8″. Cut batting for both front and back pieces.

Sew front cover to contrasting strip. You can make sharp corners by mitring, or you can make it easy and just slightly curve the corners. Sew front liner to liner strip in the same manner. Lay batting on wrong side of front cover. Place liner, wrong side against batting, onto cover. Smooth and pin so seams of both pieces match. Quilt.

Sew bottom portion of flap to contrasting strip as you did the front. Repeat for liner, wrong sides facing. Press under ½″ along edges of flap on both cover and liner.

Sandwich batting between cover and liner, aligning seams as before. To quilt, it is easier to turn the case wrong side out. Be sure not to come to the edge of the flap portion. Make sure edges are smoothly turned under on flap, and topstitch around flap.

Attach a Velcro strip across front and under flap for closing.

At top of side strip, bring the two seams together, pushing the center of the strip into the bag forming a small tuck. Take a small tacking stitch to hold the fold.

Metric Equivalents

INCHES TO MILLIMETRES AND CENTIMETRES

MM—millimetres   CM—centimetres

Inches	MM	CM	Inches	CM	Inches	CM
⅛	3	0.3	9	22.9	30	76.2
¼	6	0.6	10	25.4	31	78.7
⅜	10	1.0	11	27.9	32	81.3
½	13	1.3	12	30.5	33	83.8
⅝	16	1.6	13	33.0	34	86.4
¾	19	1.9	14	35.6	35	88.9
⅞	22	2.2	15	38.1	36	91.4
1	25	2.5	16	40.6	37	94.0
1¼	32	3.2	17	43.2	38	96.5
1½	38	3.8	18	45.7	39	99.1
1¾	44	4.4	19	48.3	40	101.6
2	51	5.1	20	50.8	41	104.1
2½	64	6.4	21	53.3	42	106.7
2	76	7.6	22	55.9	43	109.2
3½	89	8.9	23	58.4	44	111.8
4	102	10.2	24	61.0	45	114.3
4½	114	11.4	25	63.5	46	116.8
5	127	12.7	26	66.0	47	119.4
6	152	15.2	27	68.6	48	121.9
7	178	17.8	28	71.1	49	124.5
8	203	20.3	29	73.7	50	127.0

INDEX